No Brainer Relief

A CLINICALLY PROVEN PROGRAM FOR FEARS, PHOBIAS AND SOCIAL ANXIETY

Richard S. Gallagher, LMFT

R.S. Gallagher and Associates LLC
Ithaca, NY USA

Copyright © 2017 by R.S. Gallagher and Associates LLC.

All rights reserved. No part of this publication may be reproduced, stored in a retrieval system, or transmitted in any form or by any means, electronic, mechanical, recording or otherwise, without the prior written permission of the author.

Printed in the United States of America.

This publication is designed to provide accurate and authoritative information in regard to the subject matter covered. It is sold with the understanding that the publisher is not engaged in rendering psychological, financial, legal, or other professional services. If expert assistance or counseling is needed, the services of a competent professional should be sought. The publisher and author are not responsible for any specific health needs that may require medical supervision and are not liable for any damages or negative consequences from any treatment, action, application or preparation, to any person reading or following the information in this book.

R.S. Gallagher and Associates LLC
PO Box 4023, Ithaca, NY 14852-4023 USA

Author website: www.anxietycamp.com

Book Layout ©2017 BookDesignTemplates.com

No Bravery Required/ Gallagher. —1st ed.
ISBN 978-1-546301868

To the late Dr. Etta Woodward, who changed my life and inspired my own psychotherapy career. And as always, to the love of my life Colleen.

"One of the greatest discoveries a man makes, one of his great surprises, is to find he can do what he was afraid he couldn't do."

—Henry Ford

Contents

Introduction i
Acknowledgments vii

Section I. The First Steps

Understand the Enemy 1
The First Step: Mindful Awareness 13
The Mindfulness Trifecta 23

Section II. Physical Awareness

Physical Relaxation and Body Awareness 35
Breathe Your Panic Away 47

Section III. The Mental Game: You and Your Anxious Thoughts

Your Thoughts and Your Anxiety 55
Guided Imagery and Visualization 69

Section IV. Facing Your Fears Successfully

Gradual Exposure: From Thoughts to Action 79
Handling Unplanned "Life Exposures" 93
Setbacks, Stuck Points and Coaching 101

Section V. The Advanced Course

Handling Social Fears 115

Dealing with Family and Friends... 125

Beyond Your Mind: Other Approaches 135

Life Beyond Anxiety 143

Bibliography.. 147

Appendix - Worksheets

Introduction

This book is based on a simple premise: losing your fears is a lot easier than you think.

If you suffer from fears, phobias, or constant worry — particularly when these fears cripple your life — it may feel to you as if your problem is a lack of bravery. You've probably heard slogans like 'get outside of your comfort zone', or 'feel the fear and doing it anyway', and they all somehow imply that you aren't trying hard enough.

In reality, you are probably trying *too* hard.

If you are like most people, you have probably tried forcing yourself to do things you fear, because you feel you should — or because well-meaning others talked you into it. More often than not, your anxiety pushes back hard and sends you running back to the apparent safety of avoidance. This reinforces your fear, and then you mistakenly believe you will never get well.

This is the equivalent of trying to play a complex piece on the piano through brute force. You try and try again, and eventually despair that you don't seem to be getting any better. Then a music teacher comes along and shows you the technique you needed to know first - and then, with steady practice, the piece becomes easy.

It is exactly the same way with fears and phobias. You aren't weak or lacking in bravery - you simply haven't learned the right strategy. And once you know this strategy, all it takes is practice to get better. Each of the skills in this book — mindful awareness, physical relaxation, changing your thoughts, gradual exposure, and social skills — serve a similar function. Together they will help you break the code of fear.

You see, anxiety is a survival instinct. It gives you a powerful burst of nervous energy that enables you to fight or run away when you sense danger. It dates back to when we were cave people: when two cavemen heard a rustle in the bushes, the one who yawned and said, "Whatever" often got eaten, while the one who became anxious and hyper-alert survived. So when you try to fight your fears, you are fighting a powerful survival mechanism that is a sign of your intelligence. As I often tell my therapy clients, stupid people don't get anxiety.

This book will leverage your natural intelligence to help you lose your fears quickly and more easily than you may have ever imagined. It is based on evidence-based psychology and real-world experience. Most important, it lays out a step-by-step program that most people can follow — starting today — to lose their fears. Simply, easily, and with no bravery required.

Notice carefully that while I said no bravery, I did not say no *work*. The price of losing your fears will involve learning some new skills, and, more importantly, practicing them. The more you practice, the more quickly you will get well. But the steps will often be easier than you think, and well worth it.

Does bravery ever have its place? Sure. It is great for rescuing people from burning buildings, or staying alive in combat. But the most important tools for anxiety frankly lie beyond bravery. These tools work, they are extremely powerful, and they make most people start feeling a lot better.

This book combines them in a step-by-step program designed to give many people real relief from their fears.

The message of this book is that everyone can make progress toward losing their fears. Starting right now. One small, comfortable step at a time.

How This Book Came About

In 2009, as part of my graduate work in psychotherapy, I developed a program called Anxiety Camp: a low-cost, community-based program for people who suffered from fears, phobias, and other anxiety disorders. It was based around simple evidence-based concepts: mindful awareness, physical relaxation, changing your negative thoughts, gradual exposure, and communicating assertively. I taught these skills in a group program where sufferers and their families learned to become their own anxiety therapists.

It worked extremely well. Over the past five years, informal participant measures have generally showed an average 50-60 percent decrease in measured anxiety scores, even in as little as one weekend. People who went through Anxiety Camp came away with tools that helped them continue to improve thereafter. More importantly, they described this program as comfortable, easy to follow, and in many cases life-changing.

However, the real story behind this program actually came about decades earlier. Back in the 1970s, when I was in my early 20s, I spent several years living in a virtual prison. I suffered from debilitating panic attacks that eventually escalated to become a severe phobia of leaving the safety of home. For much of my early adult life, I lived in a world that was tightly circumscribed within a radius of a few blocks. Most frightening of all, no one, not even health care professionals, could tell me what was wrong with me or how to treat it.

After years of finding no relief from standard "talk" therapy, my chance encounter with a newly published self-help book in the late 1970s changed everything for me. This book, *Kicking the Fear Habit* by the late Dr. Manual J. Smith, described my problems in surprisingly accurate detail. More important, it gave these symptoms a name - agoraphobia - and described a new approach called cognitive-behavioral therapy for treating them.

I was dubious at first, but soon found a nearby therapist who was willing to try this new therapy with me, and the results were truly amazing. Just six months later I was in a suit, on a jet, flying across the country to a West Coast job interview. Soon I was able to travel freely, and it changed my life: I lived all over the United States, built a successful career as a software executive, and eventually logged over a million air miles. One year I even found myself walking on the Great Wall of China with a spouse who once believed we would never venture beyond our small neighborhood in upstate New York.

I got better in small, painless steps while learning new tools and skills to control my anxieties. Getting well was easier and more comfortable than I could have ever imagined. Then later in life, I pursued a goal that had always meant a great deal to me: becoming a psychotherapist so that I could give back to other people suffering from anxiety. Today I am a licensed therapist and regularly experience the joy of watching people get well, often for the first time in their lives.

In the years since my own recovery, we have continued to learn a great deal about how to treat anxiety. We now know that the combination of mindfulness, cognitive-behavioral therapy, and assertive communications skills is often powerful medicine for fears, phobias, and anxiety disorders. And in my own experience as a clinician, I have observed that people recover even more quickly when they use a step-by-step program with clear goals in mind.

This book presents an easy-to-understand and easy-to-follow program that will make getting well seem much easier than staying fearful. Join me and start taking the first step toward a new life free of your irrational fears!

This Book Is for You If . . .

For many people, learning to understand and work with their fears is a positive and helpful process. At the same time, everyone is different. So should you try to address your fears using a self-help book like this one? You will be most likely to benefit from this book if:

- You suffer from specific fears and phobias that interfere with your life
- You have the insight to describe what things make you uncomfortable
- You can explore your anxious thoughts on paper without getting too easily triggered
- You are able to devote at least one hour per day to practice and skill-building
- You are otherwise in relatively good health

At the same time, it is important to realize that some situations call for competent professional help. Here are a few of them:

- This book is not designed to be used with young children. Its techniques require a certain amount of logical thinking and initiative, and work best with adolescents or adults.
- Some people suffer from serious or persistent mental illnesses in addition to fears and phobias, or are easily triggered by talking about their fears. If you have been diagnosed with a severe psychiatric or dissociative disorder,

- conditions like these can make it hard to make progress on your fears unless properly treated.
- Active alcoholism or substance abuse often impedes the ability to engage your fears, and should ideally be treated as a precursor to working on fears or phobias.
- Chronic neurological conditions such as obsessive-compulsive disorder, Tourette's syndrome, bipolar disorder or others may cause people to experience fears or phobias. These disorders often require professional help, including counseling and possibly medication.
- If you are in crisis or have thoughts of suicide, your safety comes first. Call 800-273-TALK (8255) from anywhere in the United States, contact local crisis line resources if you are in another country, or seek help from your local hospital, police, or mental health professional.

It is also important to understand that emotional problems may have physical factors that cause or contribute to them. The first step in any plan to overcome fears, phobias or anxiety should be a trip to your doctor for a thorough physical examination. If you find it stressful or overwhelming to seek medical care, counseling and/or an understanding physician can often make it easier to get the help you need.

Finally, should you get help from a trained professional in addition to using this book? A good counselor, particularly one with experience in dealing with fears and phobias, has the ability to customize treatment to your individual needs. If you are experiencing high levels of distress, or suffer from mental health issues that go beyond simple anxiety, professional help is often a must. If you are seeing a clinician, feel free to show him or her this book to discuss the possibility of integrating its concepts into your treatment plan.

RICHARD S. GALLAGHER
APRIL 2017

Acknowledgments

This book is the product of nearly a decade of working with anxiety sufferers, their families, and fellow clinicians. I would like to thank the following people in my "social network" who had a role in its creation:

- To all of my clients, past and present: it has been an honor and a real pleasure to watch so many of you work successfully on losing your fears. Your hard work and victories constantly inspire me.
- To my fellow clinicians, both here in upstate New York, and those I have met nationally in the OCD and anxiety disorder community – I appreciate and cherish your fellowship and collaboration.
- To my family members for their unconditional love and support.
- To my wife and soulmate Colleen. Of all the things I have done right in my life, the best one was meeting you nearly 45 years ago. I love you.
- And finally, to everyone who struggles with fears, phobias and anxiety disorders. You are brave, intelligent, and deserve a great life. This book is for you.

Section I. The First Steps

CHAPTER 1

Understand the Enemy

Marvin is a brave police officer who breaks into a cold sweat every time he has to drive through a tunnel. Sue gets panic attacks every time she ventures more than a couple of blocks from her home. And Jon exits stage left when he sees his friends coming, because he is afraid of not knowing what to say to them. What do these three people have in common?

Intelligence.

Fear is a sign of how smart you are. It is proof that your survival instincts are working A-OK. Fear prepares us, physically and emotionally, to fight or run away in dangerous situations. You wouldn't be here today if your ancestors didn't experience anxiety when they were facing serious threats and didn't use its nervous energy to fuel action.

But here is the problem. Modern society has few hungry predators, so today these same survival instincts get misused to develop fears that limit our lives. We react emotionally and physiologically to bosses, elevators, or the threat of germs with exactly the same level of alarm as if these were life-threatening predators. So much so that according to a national survey, roughly one out of four people would be formally diagnosed with an anxiety disorder at some point in their lives.

The good news is that you can learn to change these fears. They are not your fault, they are incredibly common, and most important, they are highly treatable. This book will show you how to lose many of these fears, safely and comfortably, by learning new physical and emotional responses to these situations.

What Is Your Fear?

First, let's learn a little more about your specific fears. If you are reading this book, you probably know that you feel anxious and afraid of certain things. But you may or may not know that these fears fall into certain predictable patterns - and that in most cases, you have a lot of company.

Here are the most common types of anxiety disorders, ranked by their frequency in the population. (The number in parentheses represents the percentage of people who will be affected by each of these disorders over the course of a lifetime.)

Social Phobia (13.3%): This most common anxiety disorder involves a fear of being "on display" or trapped in social situations in front of other people. People who suffer from social phobia do not always act shy or retiring: they may appear to be affable, articulate and socially adept. But they often find interacting with people to be intensely uncomfortable.

Specific Phobias (11.3%): These are specific, individual fears directed toward situations such as heights, spiders, closed spaces, being on stage, flying - or just about anything else that you can imagine. Whatever the specific trigger, these phobias involve a fearful response that is far out of proportion to the actual threat.

> **Any Fear Can Loom Large**
>
> *Fears that may seem trivial to other people can feel overwhelming for phobia sufferers. And when they are allowed to grow and fester, these fears can eventually become life-limiting.*
>
> *For example, one person posted online about a pathological fear of mayonnaise. For him, encountering it triggered fears of food spoilage and illness. Avoiding mayonnaise may not seem like a big deal to most people, but for this person it was a major problem - because he could not even go near places like shopping malls, grocery stores, or anywhere else food might be prepared, for fear that someone might have carelessly spread even a trace amount of it.*
>
> *It is important never to judge or shame people for their fears, no matter how ridiculous they may seem to you. They all spring from the same survival instincts - and thankfully, all of them can yield to the same treatment strategies.*

Post-Traumatic Stress Disorder (PTSD) (7.8%): As the name implies, PTSD describes the deep-rooted anxiety that can spring from the aftereffects of trauma such as combat, accidents, rape, or sexual abuse. Some of its signature symptoms include hyper-arousal, feelings of dissociation and unreality, and an extreme sensitivity to specific triggering situations.

Agoraphobia (5.3%): Literally translating to "fear of the marketplace," this disorder more accurately involves a fear of being away from the safety of home or other safe places, often for fear of having a debilitating panic attack. People who suffer from agoraphobia live very geographically restricted lives, and in the worst cases may become completely housebound.

Generalized Anxiety Disorder (GAD) (5.1%): This term describes general, non-specific states of anxiety not tied to a particular fear or event. Sufferers experience frequent anxiety with or without an obvious cause, or find that they over-react to life situations in general.

Panic Disorder (3.5%): This frightening condition is marked by the sudden, rapid onset of high levels of physical anxiety and panic, including lightheadedness, high pulse rate, and feelings of unreality. People who experience panic attacks can feel like they are dying, and it is not uncommon for them to go to the hospital for fear of a real, physical problem such as a heart attack.

Obsessive-Compulsive Disorder (OCD) (2.5%): OCD is marked by intrusive anxiety-producing thoughts, ranging from fear they – or things around them – are not clean enough, to fear that they will harm other people. Sufferers manage these fears through compulsive rituals such as washing, checking, cleaning or praying, among many others.

Do any of these types of anxiety sounds like issues you experience? Are there clusters of anxiety symptoms that seem to run together for you? How do they seem connected? While these named categories can provide context to your own fears, remember that everyone is unique and has their own specific combination of symptoms.

Whatever form your own fears may take, understand that a lot of intelligent, capable people share the exact same problems that you do. If you were to meet fellow anxiety sufferers in a support group, you would discover that they aren't a bunch of strange people with three heads: they are usually nice people from all walks of life, who are often surprisingly successful in other areas of life. And even less common disorders can still affect large numbers of people - for example, if every OCD sufferer in my small town started a company together, it would be the area's second-largest employer!

Understanding the nature of your fears will be important for you on two distinct levels. First, this knowledge can help you set appropriate goals and treatment strategies. For example, someone with a simple phobia might benefit from gradual exposure, while a social anxiety sufferer may benefit even more from learning new conversation and assertiveness skills. (We will cover both of these areas later in this book.)

Even more important is cultivating an attitude of acceptance toward your fears. You are not ill or defective: you are an intelligent and worthwhile person with a common, treatable problem. As we teach you the basic skills of managing your fears throughout this book, you will discover that this attitude of acceptance will become one of the most important components of your recovery.

Tracking Your Progress

As you go through the process of working on your fears, it is often useful to take a numerical "temperature check" of how you are feeling and functioning. This is important, because your subjective feelings are not always an effective guide to how much progress you are making over time. Here are three areas you might measure:

1. Your general mood

With my own patients, I sometimes jokingly refer to what I call the "Rich Gallagher Quick Mood Assessment" – on a scale of 0 to 10, ranging from crappy to happy, how would you rate your mood today? In general, people are unhappy when they rate themselves less than a 5, fairly neutral around a 5, and relatively happy between 6 and 10.

Another brief and widely used scale for measuring your mood is the Patient Health Questionnaire (PHQ), made freely available by Pfizer, which come in forms as short as four questions. It asks you to rate how often you have been bothered by the following problems over the past two weeks, on a scale of 0 to 3 where 0 is not at all, 1 is several days, 2 is more than half the days, and 3 is nearly every day. Here is an example of the four-question version of the PHQ:

1. Feeling nervous, anxious or on edge _____
2. Not being able to stop or control worrying _____
3. Little interest or pleasure in doing things _____
4. Feeling down, depressed, or hopeless _____

This gives you a total score from 0 to 12, with your level of distress measured as none (0-2), mild (3-5), moderate (6-8) or severe (9-12). Questions 1 and 2 refer to anxiety, and questions 3 and 4 refer to depression, with scores of three or greater for either pair being positive for screening purposes.

2. Your anxiety level

When you suffer from fears, phobias, or another anxiety disorder, your general state of anxiety is another important measure to keep track of. One commonly available assessment of your anxiety is the Generalized Anxiety Disorder (GAD) scale, which consists of seven questions rated on the same 0 to 3 scale as the PHQ above. Here are the questions:

1. Feeling nervous, anxious or on edge _____
2. Not being able to stop or control worrying _____
3. Worrying too much about different things _____
4. Trouble relaxing _____
5. Being so restless that it is hard to sit still _____
6. Becoming easily annoyed or irritable _____
7. Feeling afraid as if something awful might happen _____

A total score between 5-9 is considered to be mild anxiety, between 10-14 is moderate anxiety, and 15 and above is severe anxiety. Whatever your score is, it serves as a baseline value and a starting point to work on strategies for feeling better.

3. Specific measures
Tests also exist to assess specific issues. For example:

- The Yale-Brown Obsessive Compulsive Scale (Y-BOCS) measures the severity of obsessive-compulsive disorder, and is available for public and professional use
- The Anxiety and Depression Association of America (adaa.org) offers online screening tools for specific phobias, generalized anxiety disorder, depression and other related disorders
- The Social Anxiety Institute has an online screening tool for social anxiety disorder at socialanxietyinstitute.org

Many other assessment tools are also available through health care providers, psychotherapists, and through online search. Some are freely available for use by the public, while others are licensed and administered by professionals. Whatever tools you use, these measures serve as an important way to assess your situation, and track your progress as you work toward recovery.

Fears and Phobias: Myths versus Reality

Now let's look at fears and phobias in a little more detail, and attack some of the misconceptions you might have about them. Here are some things you may not have known about your fears:

1. Fears are not governed by your personality.
Is there such a thing as fearful personality? For the most part, no. All personality types are susceptible to developing fears and phobias, and individual phobia sufferers tend to vary as much as patients in different rooms of a hospital.

Some personality traits do have some correlation to specific fears: for example, social anxiety sufferers have been shown to be significantly more introverted than the general public. Other specific types of fears are found to some degree in all personality types. Just about any person you meet could be afraid of something.

2. You can't tell who has fears or phobias by observing them.
Therapists often note that when an anxiety sufferer and his or her support person come to therapy for the first time, the therapist cannot tell which person is which until they identify themselves.

Let's compare two well-known actors: Tony Shalhoub and the late Sir Roger Moore. Shalhoub starred as fearful OCD-ridden detective Adrian Monk on television. Moore played ultra-cool spy hero James Bond, who was often portrayed getting himself out of incredibly dangerous situations without so much as a hair out of place. Which of these two actors has publicly acknowledged suffering from anxiety?

Surprisingly, the answer is Sir Roger Moore, who reportedly dropped out of a major London theatre role in 1989 because of being afraid to perform in front of a live audience. While he was capable of incredible feats in front of a movie camera, he described the experience of appearing in public to be knighted in 2003 as "the worst attack of stage fright in my life." Conversely, Monk actor Shalhoub claims not to suffer from phobias in real life.

3. Anxiety disorders are more common than athlete's foot

According to surveys, roughly 17% of people are suffering from anxiety disorders at any given time — and as we mentioned above, this figure rises to 25% over the course of a lifetime – meaning that one in four of us will at some point suffer from an anxiety disorder. There are some gender differences here as well: women are more prone to anxiety, with lifetime rates of 20% for men and 30% for women. By comparison, less than 5% of people suffer from athlete's foot!

Here are some other facts you may not have known:

- In any given year, 10 per cent of otherwise healthy adults will experience a panic attack
- Panic disorder affects more than twice as many women as men
- Anxiety disorders often occur in combination with depression or other disorders

Anxiety disorders are the most common psychiatric disorder worldwide, not counting substance abuse. This means that if you have fears, you have lots of company.

> **Famous Celebrities and Their Fears**
>
> *Whoopi Goldberg is afraid to fly. Matthew McConaughey can't go through a revolving door. Cameron Diaz often can't touch things for fear of germs. And many major league sports heroes are famous for pre-game rituals and eccentricities that they feel they must follow or else.*
>
> *Look up celebrity phobias online and you will find lots of them. Surprising? It shouldn't be. Famous people are generally very intelligent and talented, and fears often develop in people who think deeply and have strong survival instincts. And the fact that they succeed anyway is proof that people learn to function well despite their fears. Fears may seem shameful to you, but no one would bat an eyelash about them in Hollywood.*

4. People react to their fears differently

Fear affects people in different ways. You may have physical symptoms like sweating, muscle tension, or nausea. You may also have emotional responses such as agitation or panic. Or you may experience both physical and emotional responses at the same time.

Your reaction to a fearful situation will also vary based on the situation and your personality. One anxious person might try to calm down by quietly meditating — and another anxious person might find that as frustrating as watching broccoli grow. Some people might prefer a warm bath, others might want to walk around and be active, and still others might prefer to talk out their anxieties with another person. But while people react differently to their own anxieties, certain core approaches - such as mindful awareness and self-soothing techniques - can help almost everyone.

The best news of all about fears and phobias is how treatable they are. We still can't cure the common cold. But nowadays we have a surprising rate of success in treating fears and phobias. In fact, psychotherapy has a much better success rate for phobias than knee surgery does for arthritis!

This doesn't make a lot of sense to some people intellectually, because fears are so ... well ... scary. Once you understand that fear is a short-term survival reflex, however, you can understand and work with it. Because the physiology and psychology of fear are better understood than ever nowadays, we now know much better how to manage it.

This leads us to what we hope this book will do for you — give you the tools to lose your fears. We will help lead you there, one skill at a time. Let's get started!

Today's action plan

- Start looking at your fears as a common and treatable issue, not as a "flaw."
- Discover what specific kind of fears you suffer from.
- Commit to learning new skills and taking action to feel better.

CHAPTER 2

The First Step: Mindful Awareness

What if I told you that the most important thing you could do for your fears was ... nothing?

That is essentially the point of this chapter. Yes, in reality it is just a little more complex than that. But learning to be mindfully present - in other words, to *do* nothing - lies at the core of losing your fears and phobias.

This sounds easier said than done, of course. But actually, it is pretty easy. And once you get in the habit of practicing this new approach, you will probably be surprised at what a difference it makes. As long as you realize that it involves a very different way of thinking than you are used to - and, more important, as long as you are willing to practice it regularly - you will discover a powerful way to shrink your fears down to actual size.

First, let's look at what happens when most of us develop a phobia in the first place.

From Fear to Phobia

Pure, raw fear is pretty simple. It is designed to help us survive when we are confronted with danger. We see a fearful stimulus like a hungry bear and a reaction happens in short order, because of an almond-shaped part of your brain known as the *amygdala* (ah-MIG-da-la). Like a security guard at the front of a building, the amygdala processes all of your experiences. The vast majority of these experiences get waved through with no problems, but when something makes your amygdala suspicious, it raises a big, fat stop sign.

So when you are walking through the woods, taking in information through all of your senses, your amygdala is saying, "All is cool so far. Tree - check. Moss - check. Trail - check. Wind rustling through the woods - check. Bear - hey, wait a minute - BEAR!!!!"

Next, the amygdala orders your brain to pump out stress hormones, and the rest of your body springs into action - ready to run away, or even fight if needed, with a sudden burst of energy. This all happens very quickly and automatically.

Phobias, by comparison, involve a big step beyond the hungry bear scenario. They engage the thinking part of your brain. You see, normally there isn't a lot of deep thinking involved when the brain reacts to a threat. (In fact, one woman with a rare neurological disorder affecting her amygdala effectively had no fear although she was perfectly intelligent.)

You could think of a phobia in terms of what we often call "first fear" and "second fear," terms coined many years ago by the late Dr. Claire Weekes. 'First fear' is your reaction to the hungry bear: it helps you react quickly and keeps you alive in the moment. 'Second fear' mostly takes place away from the bear. It is composed of all the fearful thoughts that your thinking brain adds to this first fear before, during and after an actual encounter. For example:

- "What if I run into a bear again? Should I ever go hiking?"
- "I can't bear the thought (pun intended) of being that anxious again"
- "I need to pay close attention to every single noise I hear. You never know, it could be a bear."
- "If I can't walk outside anymore, how will this affect my relationship and my career?"

This dichotomy of 'first fear' and 'second fear' is what differentiates our basic, animal survival behavior from human anxiety disorders. Whether it is a hungry predator, a boss in a suit, or the experience of speaking in front of other people, our best interests become corrupted by our thinking patterns - often because of the very same intelligence that makes us creative and successful.

This sets many of us up for what seems like a sucker's choice. If we try to face our fears, our amygdala pushes back hard - which often sensitizes us even more. But if we keep avoiding the fear, it starts wearing a deep groove in our brain where second fear runs rampant. Our 'second fear' reinforces these 'first fear'-based behaviors. So how can we ever win? Let's look at one way out.

Introducing Mindfulness

What does the word "mindfulness" mean to you?

When I ask my therapy clients this question, I hear everything from "think happy thoughts" to "clear your mind" to "do yoga and meditate." However, the clinical definition of mindfulness is very specific: it involves learning to observe rather than react to your thoughts.

Mindful awareness is how you solve the sucker's choice we just discussed. It reprograms your amygdala by changing the script of your fearful reactions, one gradual step at a time.

Think back to when you first learned to ride a bicycle. Everything seemed unsteady and threatening at first. The bike wobbled beneath you, and you felt like you could fall at any moment.

So what did you do? You took things one small step at a time. When you felt too unsafe, you stopped the bike and planted your feet safely on the ground. As you stopped and started again, staying within your comfort zone, you became more and more present with how the rhythm of a bicycle worked. In time, the sensation of riding this bicycle came to feel totally natural to you.

Reflect back on what that process was really like. You didn't just suck it up and keep riding (unless you were a big fan of scraped knees). You didn't "feel the fear and do it anyway." Instead, you undertook a gradual process of getting your amygdala acquainted with a new and potentially fearful situation, the switch eventually flipped from unsafe to safe, and bicycles become OK.

This is exactly how you will lose your fears.

> **Mindfulness Isn't New**
>
> *People often think that mindfulness is squarely a product of the 21st century, and therefore view it as new and unproven. Or worse, they think that it is a repackaging of things like meditation or yoga, and then say, "Oh, I've tried that already." In reality, neither of these things is true.*

Mindful awareness of a fearful situation has been a component of successful treatment for many years. The problem is that, for a long time, we didn't use this term to describe it.

For example, when I was successfully treated for my own severe agoraphobia - back in the 1970s, when dinosaurs roamed the earth - I was taught to be mindfully present with the idea of being away from my home. During my office sessions, my therapist had me relax and imagine the sights, sounds and feelings of the beautiful world that surrounded me, from sunny skies to newly mown grass. Then, outside the office, I took small steps away from my cocoon of safety with a similar conscious awareness of my surroundings.

Of course, we didn't call it mindfulness back then. We simply called it therapy. But today, with decades more experience under our belts, we have a better understanding than ever of what really makes us lose our fears. And the result is a happy marriage of Eastern wisdom and Western behavioral science.

How Mindfulness Works

Mindful awareness is a subtle concept for many people that is best explained by example. First, let's look at a typical dialogue between you and your thoughts when you are afraid of something.

Thought: You are about to step in a car. Cars are dangerous.
You: Oh no! This thought is telling me to worry about getting in this car! Oh my gosh! What am I going to do?
Thought: Don't step in the car.
You: But golly Mr. Thought, I have to get to work! This is my regular carpool.

Thought: If you are going to ignore my wisdom and get in this car anyway, I am going to make you hypervigilant to all its dangers. First, go squirt some cortisol into your bloodstream so that you will be on high alert. Then pay close attention to every little noise, pothole, and intersection that you encounter. And hey, what about that guy behind the wheel - do you really trust your life with him?

So what may seem at first like an instantaneous blind panic is, in actuality, a conversation between you and your thoughts. These thoughts tell you to jack up your feelings and reactions in response to something your thought doesn't like, and you fecklessly comply.

What you are experiencing here is the classic triad of thoughts, feelings and actions, as shown in the image. You have a thought ... it then provokes a feeling ... and this feeling leads you to choose specific behaviors, such as caution or avoidance.

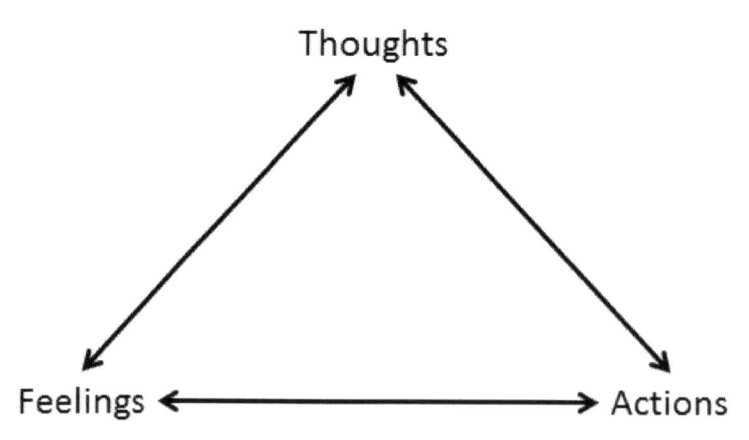

```
              Thoughts
               ↗   ↖
              /     \
             /       \
            /         \
           ↙           ↘
    Feelings ←————————→ Actions
```

Now, here is the problem with this linkage of thoughts, feelings, and actions: it is a lie.

For most people, their thoughts, feelings and actions seem inseparable. They gang up on us regularly in the name of protecting us - particularly when we experience anxiety. But in reality, each of these is a separate component - and more importantly, we can control them separately.

You already know that thoughts and feelings are separate from actions. For example, when you are running short of money, you can hold thoughts about being broke – and walk past a local bank – without robbing the bank. This is also why we do not walk into a stranger's house to use their bathroom, or help ourselves to our next-door neighbor's barbecue when we are hungry.

If you dig a little deeper, the same is often true when your thoughts or feelings involve anxiety. You may feel anxious, but your logical brain can still convince you to act contrary to this fear. For example, we are nervous about an important exam or a medical test, but we go through with it anyway, because the outcome is more important to us than our anxious feelings.

The part that gives us the most trouble, however, is the linkage between thoughts and feelings. We have a thought about something, particularly if it is fearful, and start pumping up a rich stew of neurochemicals that change the way we feel. This link is so strong that most of us take it for granted. But this link does not have to be there, and mindfulness involves learning to purposefully de-couple your thoughts and feelings - with practice.

So now, let's try a more mindful approach in this situation. Here, the dialogue goes something like this:

Thought: You are about to step in a car. Cars are dangerous.
You: I am having a thought about stepping in a car. I don't have to get rid of this thought, or even react to it. I'm just going to let this thought come and go as it pleases. After all, it is just a thought. Meanwhile, I am going to get in this car so I can get to work.
Thought: HEY! Pay attention to me! I'm trying to warn you about something dangerous!

You: This thought is trying to get my attention. I am aware of it. If it were telling me something that made logical sense to me, I could listen to it and learn from it. But I don't have to figure it out or let it trigger my emotions. By the way, it's a nice day today. Look at all that sunshine, and feel the cool breeze through the car window. Isn't it beautiful?

Thought: I'm not getting anywhere with this idiot. I'm out of here!

I'll bet that you like the second conversation a lot better than the first one. This time around we are still fully aware of our thoughts, but we are not necessarily linking them to feelings or behaviors. We are just naming them as thoughts, observing them, and learning from them - and then making our best choices from there.

This is the essence of mindful awareness. You don't try to stop your thoughts. You don't try to control them. (But you will gently give them suggestions to make them less scary - more on that a little later.) These thoughts are free to come and go as they please. But you will learn a new way of reacting to these thoughts, as you start taking steps to master your fears.

One Step at a Time

So why don't we all just start responding to our fearful thoughts this way? Simple. *Because they are much too scary.* When your amygdala is doing the driving, it does not like to be ignored - so trying to tell it that a frightening thought is "just a thought" is not always very effective. Which leads us to what is probably the most important principle of all in losing your fears:

You can do almost anything in small enough steps.

Your amygdala cannot handle a lot of fear. But it can usually handle a *little*. So when you hand it a little bit of fear - specifically a nice, easy step towards whatever it is that you fear - it can work with that. And when you teach it to be mindfully present in the face of this small, easy step, you are on your way to losing these fears entirely.

This implies that mindfulness practice takes time. It would be great if you could learn simple mindfulness techniques, and then BAM! - your phobia would disappear. In practice, however, mindfully learning to lose your fears is a lot more like dieting and exercise: you make small gains that accumulate over time, in ways that are often extremely powerful.

I often liken it to sawing a metal pipe with a hacksaw: at first, you are barely denting the surface of the pipe with your blade. But with steady progress, you start wearing a groove in the metal ... then you start cutting through the top of the pipe ... then when you hit part of the hollow middle, you literally have a breakthrough. Soon you make your way through the rest of the pipe, and it falls satisfyingly to the ground.

On the other hand, your amygdala sometimes learns faster than you think it can. So if you are, say, afraid of driving over bridges, you may not have to drive over 200 of them to lose your fear. You may be able take small steps toward one bridge, be fully present at each step, and voila: all bridges soon seem a lot less scary than they used to. For example, in recovering from my own agoraphobia, I first began mindful exposure therapy by venturing 1/4 mile away at a time in my car. But by the time I could go two miles, my next step was five miles. The next step after that was nearly 70 miles away, going shopping in the nearest major city. And soon after that, I was on a plane to visit my family 2000 miles away. Your mileage may vary (metaphor intended), but you may find your progress in fighting fear to be faster than you think – as long as you keep practicing.

This is the promise of using mindfulness to overcome fear. You do have to practice it. You do have to gently face the things you are afraid of. But more often than you think, becoming free of your fears isn't hard: rather, it is lots and lots of easy. Now, let's start learning how to put this idea into practice.

Today's action plan

- Explore the origins of your own fears.
- Break down your fearful responses into thoughts, feelings and actions.
- Start thinking about how you can be mindfully aware of your thoughts, instead of reacting to them.

CHAPTER 3

The Mindfulness Trifecta

Hopefully you now realize – if you have read the previous chapter – that one of your first goals in a fearful situation is to be mindfully aware of your thoughts and feelings.

So here you are, afraid of a situation that you are in right now. Or worrying about something that might happen in the future. What do you do with these thoughts and feelings, so you can start feeling better?

This chapter covers a three-step process for what to actually DO when you are feeling anxious, using the principles of mindful awareness that we just discussed. I call it the Mindfulness Trifecta. It is simple, easy to remember, and will really help. More important, it gives you a game plan for making long-term gains with your fears and tracking your progress. Here are the three steps:

Step 1. Observe your thoughts and feelings
Step 2. Ground yourself in the present
Step 3. Make a wise decision

Let's look at each of these three steps in detail:

Step 1. Observe Your Thoughts and Feelings

Think about hearing a song that reminds you of a favorite time in your life.

Did this song transport your thoughts back to this time and place? Or did you start moving or gesturing along with the music? What you experienced was the fusion of thought, feelings, and actions, just like we described in the previous chapter. First you had a thought about the music and the memories it brought back. Then the feelings you originally associated with that song set in. And finally, your body reacted as though you were right back in the scene it reminded you of.

Exactly the same thing happens with an anxiety disorder. Except that instead of a favorite song, you are having thoughts about something fearful – perhaps a situation you are afraid of, or a consequence you are worried about. This triggers the same fusion of feelings and actions, except they are now feelings of fearfulness, leading to physical manifestations of anxiety such as muscle tension, increase heart rate or shallow breathing. In a very real sense, you are living in your feared situation before it even happens.

So the first step in breaking the code of fear is to de-couple this fusion of thoughts, feelings and actions. How do you do this? By taking an *observer position* toward your thoughts and feelings, and *observing* and *naming* them.

Conceptually, I would like you to imagine yourself pulling up a comfortable chair, and watching these thoughts and feelings on a big movie screen in front of you. Your movie, starring you! Sit back and observe these thoughts, without judging or acting on them: after all, they are only thoughts.

Here are some examples of how to observe and name your fearful thoughts and feelings:

Before: My shoe has something on it. It could be poison! I'm going to die!
After: There is a spot on my shoe, and I am feeling somewhat uncomfortable right now.

Before: I have to talk to my teacher. He is always critical of me. I can't stand it!
After: I am thinking about what to say to my teacher, and wondering how he will react.

Before: My sister is getting married next week. I have to go, and crowds scare me!
After: I am going to a wedding next week, and thinking about what is going to happen. I am also feeling some concerns about how I will react to this.

The key here is that you are observing these thoughts and feelings, and labeling them for what they truly are: just thoughts and feelings. Thoughts that may or may not mean something. Feelings that may or may not influence how you decide to act. And you are ultimately their master.

Understand that observing your thoughts and feelings is not a magic bullet that will instantly take your fear and distress away. Rather, it is the first step in a process that will eventually help you break free of your fears. First, because the act of putting these thoughts in third person often helps calm you down. Second, it helps you develop an attitude of compassionate acceptance toward these thoughts and feelings. Ideally, you should look at these thoughts and feelings – whatever they are – and smile, point at them, and say, "Yep, that's me!"

Finally, and most importantly, this process gives you the time and space to take your mind and senses to another place, as you will see in the next two steps. So let these thoughts come and go, without judging them. Just follow the process, and see where it takes you.

> ### Don't Try to "Make It Better"
>
> *Remember the amygdala, that part of your brain we mentioned in the last chapter? The one that decides if you need to worry about something?*
>
> *Here's a little secret about it: it smells blood if you try to use positive thinking with it, and pushes back even harder. So don't try to figure out your thoughts, contradict them, or make them go away. Instead, just observe them. This will keep your amygdala much happier – and more important, keep it out of your way as you try to work on your fears.*
>
> *Let's say that you are dreading giving a presentation at work. If you try to tell yourself, "This presentation should go fine," your amygdala will respond by pointing out all the things you should worry about. And if you tell yourself that you shouldn't be feeling this way, your amygdala will be jumping up and down saying, "Yes you should!"*
>
> *Later in this book, we will discuss some more effective ways of talking back to fearful thoughts, using strategies that will make you and your amygdala both happy. And more important, how to gradually get used to fearful situations in real life. But at this point, don't try to "fix" your thoughts or make them go away. Just observe them with compassion, and let them come and go as they please.*

Step 2. Ground Yourself in the Present

Picture this: you are having a big argument with someone, and you are really upset. But then the phone rings. You answer it, and it is a repair person making an appointment to come to the house. You spend the next few minutes discussing the details of his visit with him, and then hang up the phone. How do you feel?

Most people would say that they feel less agitated than when they first picked up the phone. Why? Because you became engaged in a task that demanded all of your senses. One that pulled you out of your thoughts and into the present moment. And then your emotions followed suit.

This is precisely what the next step is in developing mindful awareness of your fears: *pull yourself out of your thoughts, and into the sights, sounds and experiences of the present moment.*

We call this grounding yourself – because in a very real sense, you are connecting yourself to the ground. You are making yourself one with your surroundings, and with your own body. And in the process, developing a further sense of detached awareness about whatever thoughts may come and go.

The classic approach to grounding yourself is to become aware of your in-breath and your out-breath, by taking slow, natural breaths from your diaphragm (in other words, your belly). We will discuss natural breathing in more detail in the next chapter, because it is also a powerful relaxation technique. But for now, simply pay attention to the natural rhythm of your breathing.

Many people find simple breath awareness to be soothing and healing. Others, however, may find it to be as boring and empty as watching broccoli grow – particularly if you have more of a "type A" personality. (Like me.) And that's OK. If breathing doesn't work for you, pay attention to the physical world around you. Notice how the food or the flowers smell. Watch people going by. Take in the colors of the sky and buildings around you. Get all of your senses into the act.

Either way, the goal of grounding yourself is to be present where you are, right here. A place where you are warm, and safe, and dry. A place where this moment is OK, and the next moment will probably be OK too. A place where you are not living in the past of your thoughts, or the future of your fears, but rather the space in time you occupy right now.

This step will not only help you feel better in the moment, but will also set the stage for the next and most important step – choosing an appropriate action.

> ***Grounding Versus Distraction***
>
> *A subtle but important point is that grounding yourself is not quite the same as distracting yourself. Distracting yourself might take the form of things like cranking up the music, or watching a movie, or immersing yourself in your work. Grounding yourself is fundamentally different from these things, because you aren't consciously shutting down your thoughts. In fact, you aren't doing anything. Instead, you are becoming fully present with your senses and the world around you.*

Step 3. Make a Wise Decision

When fear takes over, most of us react from instinct. Without even thinking, we often either make bad choices, or simply avoid the things that make us afraid. For example, we may react to a stressful situation by reaching for the bottle, or letting our partner do all the shopping for us.

Our goal here is to replace this instinct with thoughtful choice. I call this "making a wise decision." Instead of blindly following a fearful thought, we pause, observe the thought and its feelings, ground ourselves, and then *choose* our next behavior.

What do we mean by a "wise decision?" It means any behavior that is thoughtfully chosen, and not simply a reaction to your thoughts. This is important, because developing a sense of choice and control will be an essential element of losing your fears. Here are the three components of a wise decision:

A wise decision is not rushed. A subtle but key point here is that the decision itself is not the most important thing – the most important thing is breaking the automatic fusion of thoughts, feelings and actions. So stop, breathe, and take the time to make choices about your actions.

A wise decision is neither "right" nor "wrong." Wise decisions do NOT automatically imply facing your fears. In fact, not facing them may sometimes be the best choice in the moment. Either way, it is your decision.

Let's say, for example, that you have contamination fears and notice a red spot on your shirt. Sometimes a wise decision may be to simply live with this red spot, and try to get used to it so that you are less fearful in the future. Or you may decide to delay reacting to it, to start practicing being less reactive. Or you may decide that you have an exam or a big presentation tomorrow, and that ignoring this spot will keep you up obsessing all night – so you choose to clean the shirt. ALL of these are wise decisions, guided by your own unique situation and your own judgment.

A wise decision is uniquely yours. Every time you stop and make a wise decision in a fearful situation, you are reinforcing your own sense of personal choice. We refer to this as having a sense of *agency*. In general, the more agency you have, the better – because emotional distress springs from feeling like a helpless victim of circumstance, and emotional relief springs from having choice, control and agency. Even in difficult situations.

> **Having Agency in the Worst of Times**
>
> *When the horror of the 9/11 terrorist attacks played out on television screens all over the United States, how did people react? In many cases, they gave blood. Lines to donate were hours long in some places, and donors included everyone from average citizens to nearly every member of the U.S. Congress. While ironically much of this donated blood was eventually discarded – because it has a short shelf life, and donations far outstripped the need – people felt it was important to be able to do something in the midst of tragedy, and in many cases this helped them to feel better.*

Pulling It All Together

Observing your thoughts and feelings, grounding yourself in the present moment, and making a wise decision are much more than just helpful tips: they are an evidence-based strategy based on solid research in mindful awareness. And with practice, they can become part of your normal way of thinking.

Again, these three steps are not magic bullets that instantly take your fear and anxiety away. Rather, they are steps in the right direction. They represent a new way of thinking about fearful situations that will help you in the present moment, as well as a base for losing these fears in the long term. Think of them as a foundation for the most important steps in becoming anxiety free: changing your fearful thoughts, and using gradual exposure to re-experience fearful situations, both of which we will cover next in the chapters to come.

Today's action plan

- The next time you feel anxious about a feared situation, stop and observe your thoughts and feelings.
- Find your own personal way to ground yourself in the present: breath awareness, body awareness, or getting in touch with your senses and surroundings.
- Don't just react to your thoughts and feelings – instead, pause, reflect, and then make a wise decision.

Section II. Physical Awareness

CHAPTER 4

Physical Relaxation and Body Awareness

Now that you are starting to learn how to think when you are anxious, or facing a fearful situation, the next step in your recovery is to learn how to soothe yourself physically – using the powerful natural resources we all have in our own bodies, and have had for thousands of years.

We all have a very strong mind-body connection, and learning to calm your body will have a strong beneficial impact on your mind as well. It is not the only tool you need – otherwise everyone could cure their anxiety disorders by taking a nice, hot bubble bath! To lose fears and phobias, we also need to learn how to think differently about the things we fear, and gradually re-experience them in a different light. But physical self-soothing techniques are an important and necessary part of your toolkit for overcoming your fears.

An important part of this mind-body continuum is that you cannot be anxious and totally physically relaxed at the same time. This is why we often medicate anxiety through prescription medication, and sometimes self-medicate it through alcohol or drugs. All of these can affect either our state of relaxation, or the brain chemistry that controls this relaxation. But the good news is that there are tools we can learn that help us tap into our own internal states of relaxation – with no side effects.

In this chapter, we will discuss three strategies you can use to calm yourself down, both in fearful situations and in everyday life:

- Diaphragmatic or "belly" breathing
- Progressive muscle relaxation
- Body scan or autogenic relaxation

The next chapter will also discuss a very specific and powerful technique for stopping a panic attack by changing the way you breathe. But here, our focus will be on soothing and calming the mind and body. Let's begin.

Diaphragmatic Breathing

Breathing is as natural as … well, breathing, right? Not always.

Stress often leads us to take in short, shallow breaths from our upper chest. This upsets the balance of oxygen and carbon dioxide in our bloodstream, which in turn can lead us to feel physically anxious and out of control. This causes us to feel dizzy, lightheaded, increases the lactic acid concentrations in our muscles, and eventually triggers our "suffocation alarm" that we are not getting enough air to breathe.

However, we can control these physical sensations by learning how to breathe properly. Breathing slowly and naturally from our diaphragm – the smooth wall of muscle between our chest and our abdomen, at the base of our lungs – helps to calm us and clear our minds. Here is why:

- Natural, relaxed breathing comes from our diaphragm, not our chest.
- Slowing down our rate of breathing allows us to better utilize the oxygen in the air we breathe.
- Proper breathing helps regulate the rest of our physical functions.

Diaphragmatic or "belly" breathing is a skill that we can learn and employ on demand to reduce our symptoms of anxiety. When we do this, we are reconnecting with the way all mammals naturally breathe when they are safe and out of danger, a state known scientifically as *eupnea*. In the figure below, notice how your diaphragm – the muscle wall at the bottom of your lungs – pulls air into your lungs as you inhale. When you exhale, the reverse happens and your diaphragm naturally pushes air out of your lungs.

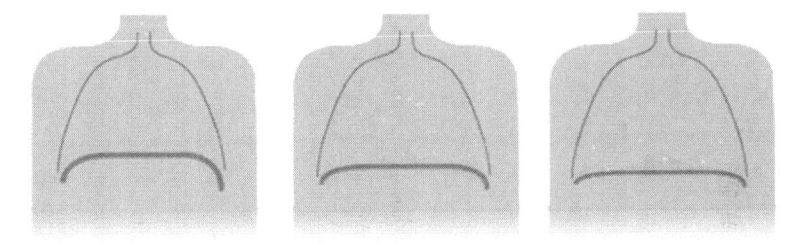

Figure 4-1. Inhaling using your diaphragm, as shown from left to right[1].

Here is one sample procedure for diaphragmatic breathing, courtesy of the United States Veteran's Administration[2]:

---

[1] Source: John Pierce, Wikimedia Commons, https://commons.wikimedia.org/wiki/File:Diaphragmatic_breathing.gif
[2] U.S. Department of Veterans' Affairs, "Relaxation Exercise: Deep Breathing," http://www.va.gov/vetsinworkplace/docs/em_eap_exercise_breathing.asp

1. Sit comfortably or lie down.
2. Place one hand on your stomach and one hand on your chest.
3. Breathe in slowly through your nose.
4. Feel your stomach expand as you inhale. If you are breathing from the stomach, the hand on your chest shouldn't move.
5. Focus on filling up your lower lungs with air.
6. Slowly exhale, releasing all the air out through your mouth.
7. Use your hand to feel your stomach fall as you exhale.
8. Practice breathing four to six breaths per minute (about one full inhale and exhale per 10-15 seconds).

Repeat this procedure up to 10 times. Most people experience a sense of calm and peace as they focus on their in-breath and their out-breath. However, if at any time during this exercise you feel lightheaded or uncomfortable, simply stop and resume normal breathing. With practice, we can learn to breathe from our diaphragm as a matter of habit. Make it a point to regularly put one hand on your chest and the other on your abdomen, and become aware of your regular breathing habits.

> **Managing Your Energy Level Through Breathing**
>
> *Another diaphragmatic breathing exercise for raising oxygen levels in the blood and the energy in the body is to take several negative breaths, immediately followed by an equal number of positive breaths. During negative breaths, you inhale, immediately exhale and then hold your breath for a short time. The emphasis is in keeping your lungs empty. Negative breaths reduce the oxygen in your blood. During positive breaths, you inhale, hold your breath, and then exhale. The emphasis is in keeping your lungs full. Positive breaths increase the oxygen in your blood. (Source: soultherapynow.com)*

The good thing about breathing exercises is that you can do them anytime, anywhere. Best of all, they can be done unobtrusively – even in the middle of a meeting! This makes them an important part of the toolkit that you bring with you into a fearful situation, or any time that you need to take a break from stressful feelings.

Progressive Muscle Relaxation

Next, we will look at a very powerful technique that we can use to physically relax, particularly when we are anxious, fearful, or cannot sleep. Progressive muscle relaxation, first described in the 1920s by Dr. Edmund Jacobson, harnesses the natural process of tensing and releasing our muscles to create a deep state of relaxation.

As we discussed earlier, we cannot be anxious when our muscles are fully relaxed. In fact, this is how many popular anti-anxiety medications such as Klonopin and Xanax work - they relax our muscles, and in fact are often prescribed for muscular problems such as back spasms as well as anxiety. Alcohol also has a similar effect, which is why people often use it to self-medicate, although it carries with it a host of other health problems and the risk of addiction. This is why learning to deeply relax our own muscles is one of the best physical strategies we can learn for managing our own anxiety.

The key principle behind progressive muscle relaxation is that muscles relax as a response to being tensed first – and progressively tensing and releasing each of your key muscle groups is the key to achieving a deep overall state of relaxation.

Try a small experiment first. First, take a slow, deep breath from your diaphragm, as we described above. Then, if it doesn't hurt to do so, make a fist and tense up your forearm as hard as you comfortably can. Hold this tension for five seconds and observe how it feels. Then exhale and release all of the tension in your arm, letting it hang limp.

Now, how does the arm you just tensed feel? And how does this feeling compare with your other arm? Ideally, the arm you tensed should feel warm, tingly and relaxed. Get in touch with this feeling – with practice, it will improve. This is ultimately the way you want your entire body to feel, after spending perhaps 15 minutes working your way up from your feet to your head.

I personally find that it helps to silently say the word "RELAX" as you breathe in and tense each muscle group, and then say "LET GO" as you breathe out and let these muscle groups go limp. Step by step, go through each of the following muscle groups:

- Toes – curl them towards you as you tighten them
- Feet and ankles – tighten these gradually. Note: if you start to get a cramp in the arch of your feet, press them flat against the floor.
- Calves – point your toes away from or towards you as you tighten these
- Thighs – squeeze both thighs together
- Buttocks – clench your cheeks together
- Lower back – gently and gradually tense your lower back muscles, and be cautious if you suffer from lower back pain
- Middle and upper back – gently arch your back to get in touch with these muscles, which are a key to relaxing your entire body
- Lower abdomen – tense the smooth muscles in your belly
- Chest and upper abdomen – bring your shoulders to the front to help tense these muscles
- Shoulders – lift your shoulders toward your ears as you tense them
- Upper arms

- Forearms and hands – make a fist as you tense these muscles
- Neck – gently rotate your head as you tense your neck muscles
- Face – make a big smile, hard enough to feel the corners of your mouth tensing up
- Eyes – close your eyes tightly
- Forehead – raise your eyebrows and try to get in touch with those hard-to-reach muscles in your upper scalp

By the time you finish this exercise, you should feel substantially more relaxed, physically AND mentally. And these gains get a lot better with practice, as you learn to get in touch better with each of your skeletal muscle groups. In return for taking 15 boring minutes out of your life, you gain many of the benefits that most people only experience through medication – and a natural state of calm that you can produce for yourself whenever you need it.

Another excellent way to learn progressive muscle relaxation is to be guided by an audio exercise. Several excellent ones exist and can be found online, ranging from paid exercises available via download and CD, as well as free exercises available through web sites and video channels such as YouTube. One very good – and free – resource is a full 18-minute progressive muscle exercise available online at the University of Texas' Mind-Body Lab (cmhc.utexas.edu/mindbodylab.html).

Once you are familiar with the basics of progressive muscle relaxation, you can experiment with doing shorter versions of this exercise, tensing and releasing larger groups of muscles at the same time. For example, you can tense your legs, feet and buttocks together, your back, chest, and arms in a second group, and finally your shoulders and head. This will allow you to use these skills on demand whenever you need them – for example, as a public speaker, I often do a quick whole-body relaxation exercise before I go on stage to speak to a large audience.

> **Progressive Muscle Relaxation and Sleep**
>
> *If you have insomnia or trouble sleeping, progressive muscle relaxation is an excellent way to help yourself drift off or get back to sleep.*
>
> *If you use it for this purpose, be sure to work your way up from your feet to your head, and tense and release your scalp and facial muscles last. Many people do not realize that relaxing your scalp muscles, which take practice to get in touch with, are your body's signal to switch off and go to sleep. This is because much of our cognitive processes are tied up in our facial muscles during our normal waking hours.*
>
> *Using PMR to get to sleep can be particularly useful for situational bouts of insomnia, such as long distance travel, jet lag or shift changes. Try it and see if it helps you sleep better!*

We all have the ability to get in touch with our muscle groups and physically relax them. Progressive muscle relaxation techniques can be learned and practiced, and give us powerful benefits including lower anxiety levels, less fear in difficult situations, and less unnecessary physical tension during our normal daily activities.

> **Some Important Precautions for Progressive Muscle Relaxation**
>
> - *Consult your doctor before doing progressive muscle relaxation if you suffer from high blood pressure or heart disease, as these exercises can cause a temporary increase in blood pressure.*

- *Progressive muscle relaxation can aggravate "trigger points" of muscle pain and stiffness for some people. Never tense your muscles to the point where it hurts to do so.*

- *Rarely, some people can also experience relaxation-induced anxiety, or stress resulting from the release of emotions bound up in physical tension. Stop doing muscle relaxation exercises if you notice any negative emotional reactions. (Source: Wikieducator.com)*

Body Scan or Autogenic Relaxation

Progressive muscle relaxation, as we have described above, is often the gold standard for creating a deep, physical state of relaxation. But it does have two drawbacks.

- First, it takes a lot of time. Doing a full progressive muscle relaxation exercise from head to toe can often take 15-20 minutes or more, although you can quickly reach many of your major muscle groups in a shorter time frame.
- Second, it isn't always appropriate for everyone, particularly in cases of physical injury that where tensing and releasing your muscles is contraindicated, or conditions such as high blood pressure or cardiac issues.

Fortunately, you can obtain many of the benefits of muscle relaxation by practicing autogenic relaxation, where you simply imagine peace and relaxation flowing to individual body parts. This is also sometimes referred to as a body scan, because you scan each major part of your body to eventually relax them. Consider some of the following strategies for dissipating the tension in your body:

- Imagine directing your breathing toward parts of your body, and feel the tension slip away from each major muscle group as you focus on it.
- Starting from your feet, and rising slowly upward from there, imagine the tension being forced out of your body through a hole in the top of your head.
- Focus on each part of your body in turn, and feel it sink into the chair, couch or mattress where you are resting.

Autogenic relaxation exercises are generally much shorter than progressive muscle relaxation. They also have the added advantage that you can do them anytime or anywhere, including in public. For many people, they are an easy and natural way to induce physical relaxation.

Anxiety is Physical as well as Emotional

Anxiety is a strong survival instinct that affects us physically as well as emotionally. It prepares our bodies to fight or run away by making the following things happen physically:

- Blood flow is directed toward the extremities, to strengthen them. This causes gastric problems such as "butterflies" in our stomach, nausea, or diarrhea.
- Cortisol and adrenaline are pumped into our bloodstream, causing the heart to beat faster.
- We start taking short, shallow breaths to keep up with the oxygen requirements of the increased blood flow
- Our immune system shuts down to divert resources to the threat at hand.

All of this is very helpful if we are confronted by a hungry predator or a hostile gang. But it isn't helpful at all when we trigger this reflex constantly with irrational fears - it wears our body down to be on a state of constant alert. But we can use our awareness of our bodies to control our physical reactions to stress. By using tools such as breathing, progressive muscle relaxation and body scanning, you can leverage the survival resources of your body to help you have less anxiety, fewer physical symptoms, and a faster path toward dealing with fearful situations in your life.

Today's Action Plan

- Anxiety involves physical reactions as well as emotional ones. Start practicing ways to lower your anxiety by taking steps to control your physical reactions.
- Become aware of your breathing patterns, and learn how diaphragmatic or "belly" breathing can create beneficial changes in the balance of oxygen and carbon dioxide in your bloodstream and help you feel more relaxed.
- If appropriate to your physical situation, practice progressive muscle relaxation or autogenic relaxation, and learn how to create a deep physical sense of calm.

CHAPTER 5

Breathe Your Panic Away

Do you ever experience that sudden, frightening, out-of-control sensation that you are going to slip into a state of panic? What you are experiencing is actually a powerful survival trait that, throughout history, gave us the strength to fight or run away — one that also leads many of us to misinterpret our physical sensations, breathe and react the wrong way, and let panic spiral out of control.

This chapter will teach you how to recognize the signs of a panic attack and use a simple breathing technique to stop them. It comes to us courtesy of my good friend and colleague Dr. Joseph Strayhorn, a Drexel University professor and child psychiatrist who has written extensively about managing anxiety. Try it, and you will learn that you have much more control over panic than you think.

What is a Panic Attack?

The Mayo Clinic defines a panic attack as "a sudden episode of intense fear that triggers severe physical reactions when there is no real danger or apparent cause." To a sufferer, a panic attack can feel like the end of the world. It often seems to come completely out of the blue, and surround you with an overwhelming sense of impending doom. People sometimes mistake its symptoms for a physical problem such as a heart attack, and rush themselves to a hospital emergency room.

Panic attacks can have a wide range of causes. They could be caused by a buildup of emotional pressures, the aftermath of trauma, or even too much coffee in sensitive individuals. Whatever their origin, they often cause a physical and mental spiral that goes something like this:

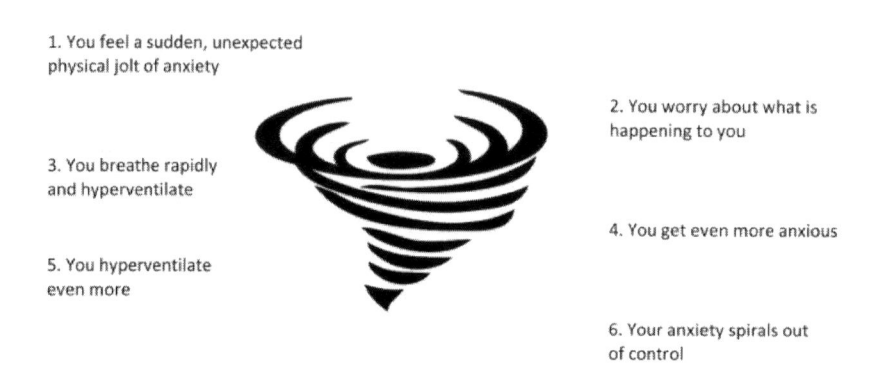

1. You feel a sudden, unexpected physical jolt of anxiety

2. You worry about what is happening to you

3. You breathe rapidly and hyperventilate

4. You get even more anxious

5. You hyperventilate even more

6. Your anxiety spirals out of control

In other words, the physical sensations of sudden anxiety cause emotional reactions that make you even more fearful. Your body then responds by making the panic even worse, until it reaches a crescendo. This horrible spiral continues until you reach a point of exhaustion, and can continue to wash over you in waves of recurring panic.

Meanwhile, a lot of uncomfortable physical sensations are happening to you at the same time:

- You may feel lightheaded and unsteady
- Your arms and legs may feel like they are made of rubber
- You may be nauseous or feel like your "guts are on fire"

- Your eyesight may be blurry
- You may feel like you are not getting enough air

Why would any sane person ever put themselves through this kind of torment, even subconsciously? Simply put, to survive. All of these awful feelings give you a powerful burst of nervous energy designed to help you fight or outrun danger. These sensations are caused by oxygen rushing into your bloodstream as a result of hyperventilation, and blood rushing from your extremities to your core.

The problem is that in this modern world, you probably aren't about to fight someone or run away. So from an evolutionary standpoint, panic is like being all dressed up and ready to go — to the wrong party. Now, let's look at how to harness your breathing to stop these reactions.

Stopping a Panic Attack with Your Breathing

So now let's look at the last of these physical effects that we mentioned: the feeling that you are not getting enough air. This is truly the big lie of a panic attack: in reality, you are breathing too much, and as a result you have too little carbon dioxide (CO_2) in your bloodstream. And as you are furiously trying to breathe in more, in preparation to fight or run away, this continues to expel CO_2. But since you usually don't do either, you instead feel lightheaded and panicky.

This means that there is one fundamental rule for stopping a panic attack in its tracks: **slow down your breathing**. In other words, replace the rapid, shallow breaths of panic with slow, purposeful breaths that are driven by your natural need for air. Doing this will quickly restore the balance of carbon dioxide and oxygen in your bloodstream to normal levels, and let you feel grounded again.

How do you know how much to slow down your breathing? Easy — your body will tell you. All you need to do is get in touch with the natural sensation of air hunger that leads us all to draw an inward breath. And more important, understand that this sensation is fundamentally different from the rapid breathing that accompanies a panic attack.

Here is a simple exercise you can use to learn how to breathe through a panic attack:

> *1) Relax and let your breath out, slowly and naturally, breathing out from your diaphragm.*
>
> *2) Don't breathe in again until air hunger tells you it is time to breathe in. Don't make it a point to hold your breath, but rather get in touch with this natural sensation of air hunger. Sense it, feel it, and then let it guide you toward when to breathe in again.*
>
> *Notice first of all that air hunger is not generally an anxious feeling unto itself. It is just a need for oxygen, culminating in the urge to breathe in. Then when you do breathe in, observe how quickly this sense of air hunger dissipates. Relief from air hunger is fundamentally as close as your next breath.*
>
> *Second, notice the difference between this sense of air hunger versus the artificial and deceptive sense that you are "not getting enough air" when you start to have a panic attack. The former is driven by a natural physical need for more oxygen, while the latter is a false emotional belief.*
>
> *3) Now continue breathing slowly and naturally.*

> *A good rule of thumb is to see if you can wait 20 seconds after you exhale to take your first inward breath after you first experience sensations of panic. Again, it is not necessary to hold your breath; rather, just maintain a thoughtful awareness of when your natural sense of air hunger tells you to breathe in.*

This technique is very powerful, and it works best when you try it yourself before you have a panic attack: that way you will know how it works, how to cue your breathing, and what physical sensations to expect. Here is one way to practice:

- Take several rapid, deep breaths from your upper chest, in quick succession — between five and ten such breaths. This will normally induce a very mild state of hyperventilation.
- Wait about 30 seconds, breathing normally, and notice the sensations that come with this mild hyperventilation, such as a slight sensation of lightheadedness and tingling of the extremities. These are a very small-scale example of the same physical sensations you experience with a panic attack.
- Now slow down your breathing as described above, exhaling deeply and letting air hunger guide your next inward breath. Then continue to breathe slowly and naturally.

Notice how quickly you start to feel grounded again? Most people start to feel better within less than a minute of slowing down their breathing. With practice, you can calmly and comfortably stop most panic attacks in their tracks — just by changing the way you breathe.

Dr. Strayhorn makes the point that some of the breathing techniques promoted in the past for managing panic — such as breathing in and out of a paper bag, or counting your breaths

— are a poor substitute for the real solution, which is to simply *slow down your breathing*. His own book *A Programmed Course in Anxiety Reduction and Courage Skills* (Psychological Skills Press, 2012) discusses the physiology of this in much more detail for those who would like to take a deeper dive into this approach.

Panic attacks are among the most frightening experiences most of us will ever encounter — and ironically, also one of the most treatable. While it may be helpful to understand and work with feelings that lead to panic attacks, and in some cases medication or counseling may help reduce your tendency to panic, the actual panic attack itself is often very well-defined and physical in nature. By learning to control our breathing, most of us can learn to quickly put an end to panic, and in turn start losing our fears of having these attacks.

Today's Action Plan

- Understand that panic attacks are often caused by a correctable imbalance of carbon dioxide and oxygen in your bloodstream
- Practice experiencing the sensation of "air hunger" as outlined in this chapter, and discover how quickly it is cured by simply breathing in
- Practice a small, safe sample of the sensations of hyperventilation, as discussed earlier, and learn to stop these sensations by breathing more slowly

Section III. The Mental Game: You and Your Anxious Thoughts

CHAPTER 6

Your Thoughts and Your Anxiety

Now we are going to turn our attention to the thing that really causes most of your fears: your mind. Because left to its own devices, your mind is a bad storyteller that excels at telling you scary – but inaccurate – stories. Here we are going to look at how you start changing these stories to be more rational, more actionable, and less scary – which in turn, will make it much easier to face your fears.

First, it is important to understand that, believe it or not, anxiety is not caused by things that happen to you. It is caused by your reactions to what happens -- and most of these reactions are wrong! We all have an innate tendency to exaggerate the worst of any situation, and then react to these exaggerations. By learning to understand and examine our response to a situation, we can greatly reduce the amount of stress we feel.

Three steps happen in our thoughts to create stress. Legendary psychologist Albert Ellis, one of the fathers of cognitive-behavioral therapy (the approach on which this book is based), called this the A-B-C:

1. An **A**ctivating event happens.
Example: A car swerves towards us as we cross the street.

2. We interpret this event through our **B**eliefs.
Example: "That car swerved towards me because they don't like the way I am dressed."

3. The **C**onsequences: we act on these beliefs, and not the event.
Example: Yelling out "You jerks! I'll get you!" as they drive off. (In reality, they were trying to avoid something in the road and weren't paying attention to you at all.)

While we often cannot change the Activating event, we can examine – and possibly change – the incorrect Beliefs that cause our distress. Whatever the situation is. By responding assertively to the real situation, and not our worst fantasies about them, we help manage our emotional reactions, and bring the situation more quickly to a solution. Now, let's look at how to do this.

Cognitive Restructuring: A Lofty Term for Changing How You Think

You are a smart person. So you already know that you can't just snap your fingers and change your thoughts. If you could, you probably wouldn't ever suffer from anxiety!

But with some practice, you actually can change the way you react to these anxious thoughts – and eventually, change the way you think, so that you are less anxious in the first place. How? Simple. *Change the language you use to talk to yourself.*

Think about it. If you smile sweetly at your partner and say, "Honey, I would really love it if you would take out the garbage," you might get one reaction. But if you scowl at them and bark, "I always have to remind you to take out the garbage! You are a terrible person! And I demand that you take the garbage out right now!", you will probably get a very different reaction.

The very same principle is at work when you talk to yourself. And sadly, most of us use language with ourselves that we would never dream of using with someone else. We criticize and shame ourselves about our anxieties, and we exaggerate anxious situations until they loom in our minds as scary monsters. Here as well, changing the words can create a very different reaction.

So here is a simple, three-step process for changing these thoughts:

Step 1. Write them down
Step 2. Look for common distortions (e.g. errors in thinking)
Step 3. Rewrite them so the distortions are no longer true.

Then start using this new language with yourself, and see how it makes you feel. At the very least, you will have a better perspective on anxious situations, before you start practicing behavioral strategies such as gradual exposure therapy (which will discuss in chapters to come). At best, you may experience a change in viewpoint that takes the fear away entirely. I have seen both happen as a therapist – but either way, this is a necessary first step to working with your fears.

Step 1 is deceptively simple, but critically important. Freezing thoughts on paper is what allows you to work on these thoughts in the cold light of day. This step will give you a perspective that you would never have just by letting these thoughts run through your mind. Moreover, you will see how you really talk to yourself – and in all likelihood, you would be shocked if anyone was as critical or judgmental with anyone else.

Step 2 is where the real work comes in: take these thoughts on paper, and look for what we call *cognitive distortions* – a fancy clinical term for errors in the way that we think about a situation. There are many detailed summaries of common cognitive distortions in the literature. I personally find, however, that it is much easier to do this process if we boil these down into a very short list. To me, most cognitive distortions fit into one of three broad categories:

- **Exaggeration**. You are exaggerating the situation in some way – by using closed-minded black-and-white thinking, by not seeing the good as well as the bad aspects of a situation, or by dramatizing the situation or its consequences.
- **Prediction**. You are predicting a future that may or may not actually happen – or presume someone dislikes you for reasons that may or may not be accurate.
- **Expectation**. You have unrealistic expectations of how you or others should feel or react.

Here are some examples of each of these cognitive distortions:

Exaggeration	"I can't take this anymore"
	"This situation is very threatening"
Prediction	"Things are going to turn out horribly"
	"She is going to be very upset with me."
Expectation	"I should be strong and never feel anxious"
	"My mother-in-law should treat me better."

These statements are not only scary sounding, they also aren't completely true. At best, they are perhaps half-true. Or perhaps not even true at all. But we MAKE these statements scary, because we believe that fear will keep us safe. And it is in changing these statements that we start changing our fear.

Step 3 is simple – but not easy. You just rewrite these statements so that these cognitive distortions are no longer true. Then start using these new statements when you talk to yourself or others.

A little coaching is in order here. Cognitive restructuring does *not* involve positive thinking. In fact, your amygdala – that part of your brain that tells you whether to worry about something – smells blood when you use positive thinking, and pushes back even harder to protect you. Instead, you need to come up with realistic statements that your amygdala will shake hands with – but are less scary. And ideally, replace these scary, helpless thoughts with skills and choices.

The simple part is taking these cognitive distortions, and using them as a guide to change your language:

- If you are using exaggeration, you need to describe the situation neutrally and accurately.
- If you are using prediction, you must acknowledge both the positive and negative possibilities – with a game plan for either outcome.
- If you are using expectation, you need to align these expectations with reality.

Let's try this with the above examples of distorted statements:

	Distorted statements	**Realistic statements**
Exaggeration	"I can't take this anymore" "This situation is very threatening"	"This stinks, but I've handled it before." "This situation is unpleasant, but I should survive it."
Prediction	"Things are going to turn out horribly" "She is going to be very upset with me."	"Things might work out, and they might not. Here are the factors I can control. And here is what I will do if things don't turn out as I hoped. "I will communicate as best as I can with her, and try to soothe her feelings. If she is unhappy, I will respond authentically and non-defensively."
Expectation	"I should be strong and never feel anxious" "My mother-in-law should treat me better."	"No one is made of steel. I am who I am. And I do feel anxious sometimes." "My mother-in-law predictably reacts in certain ways. Here is how I will handle these reactions."

Note carefully that these realistic statements are not cheery and sunny – they are *realistic*. They acknowledge what is really and truly difficult about a situation, and couple these authentic beliefs with a game plan for managing the situation. It is this combination of accuracy and action that helps to shrink your fears down to actual size, before you start working with them.

> **Exercise: Spot the Cognitive Distortions!**
>
> *Take the following five examples and see how many cognitive distortions you can spot:*
>
> *1. You are in high school, and your friend Margie wants you to go to the movies Tuesday night. You are upset because she went out with other friends Saturday night, when everyone else goes out. You feel like you're "second best" and that she settles for you when no one else is available.*
>
> *2. You invite Uncle Charlie to go on a vacation to Florida with your family. He replies, "No way! Did you see that plane crash in the paper last week? You'll never get me up in one of those things again!"*
>
> *3. You work at Dairy Whizz, and your boss scowled at you tonight and said that you put too much whipped cream on a customer's hot fudge sundae. Now you are lying awake in bed unable to sleep.*
>
> *4. You are the president of a major local bank. Your vice-president comes up to you one afternoon, showing a report that shows his division's profits are down. He is shaking and red-faced as he exclaims, "These people are out to get me! They will stop at nothing until they get me fired!"*
>
> *5. You are seven years old, and last week a bully shoved you and made fun of you on the playground you've been going to all summer. Now you won't go back to the playground any more.*

Now, let's explore two concepts that will make cognitive restructuring a lot easier, and in turn make your fears a lot less scary. The first is reframing, and the other is agency.

Using Reframing

Did you know that soldiers in an army do not actually shoot at anyone? This is because in the military, they often refer to the process of firing at enemy soldiers as "servicing the target."

What you are seeing here is an example of reframing, where something is worded in ways that are less harsh or emotional.

Sometimes reframing can be very beneficial – such as the case where degrading terms like "mentally retarded" are replaced with more accurate ones such as "learning disabled". Other times it can be deceptive – such as calling a tiny, cramped apartment "cozy" in an advertisement, or referring to shooting someone as "servicing the target." Here, we are only going to use the good form of reframing, to make your anxious thoughts seem a lot less scary!

When you are dealing with anxiety, reframing can be your best friend. Here is why:

- Reframing can turn situational anxiety into excitement.
- Reframing can turn fear into appropriate caution.
- Reframing can turn "bad" or "scary" people into human beings you can understand and relate to.
- Reframing can turn failure into learning experiences
- Reframing can turn avoidance into experimentation.

Intrusive Thoughts: A Different Situation

Some people who suffer from obsessive-compulsive disorder experience unwanted, intrusive thoughts. For example, they may suddenly feel overwhelmed by a thought that they might harm their spouse or child, have inappropriate sexual feelings, or do something irrational.

This is not the same as people who have urges to do these things. Intrusive thoughts do not make a person more likely to act on these things. A good litmus test is how much distress these thoughts cause: if you find these thoughts to be extremely disturbing, your problem is not likely a desire to act on them, but rather a survival instinct gone haywire.

In cases like these, trying to reframe these thoughts can turn into a reassurance ritual, and can actually make things worse. Rather, the goal here is to learn to ignore and disregard these thoughts rather than react to them, much like people learn to tune out the traffic noise in a big city.

Reframing involves replacing harmful and judgmental observations with neutral and factual ones, which in turn create a basis for new ways to look at uncomfortable situations. Here are some ways to do this:

1. Do this on paper, not in your head. When you put your old and new thoughts on paper, you do two important things: you explore them in detail, and you "commit" to them in a way that does not happen when you simply think about them.

2. Do not try to "negate" your anxious thoughts. If you tell yourself a thought is silly, or simply won't happen, this will cause one small problem - you won't believe yourself! Instead, your job is to find the truth in your fearful thoughts, and then reword this truth in ways that are less scary. For example:

Old thought: If I don't check the door again, something bad will happen.
New thought: I have an urge to check things caused by my OCD, not by anything in reality.

Old thought: Mark seems pretty upset. He must be mad at me.
New thought: I have no idea why Mark is upset. I'll ask him.

3. Replace negative descriptions with neutral and factual ones. This technique is particularly effective when you have people or situations that frighten you. This is not the same as "thinking happy thoughts" - rather, it is how to describe people or situations in the most positive accurate way possible. Picture yourself as an academic researcher exploring these difficult situations for a research paper, instead of a frightened victim. For example:

Old thought: My boss is a jerk and I am afraid to confront her.
New thought: This boss is very frank and results-oriented, so I will need to acknowledge her concerns if I want to talk with her productively.

Old thought: These parties always put me on edge, given my social anxiety.
New thought: Because I am thoughtful rather than verbal, I need to take steps to be comfortable in social settings like a party, like talking one-on-one with familiar people.

4. Choose a different language. Replace "catastrophizing" words and phrases with ones that are more accurate – but still completely valid. Here are some examples of words to lose versus words to use:

Words to lose	Words to use
I'll have to	I may choose to
I can't	I might not want to
The worst	Not as pleasant as I would like
Unbearable	Annoying
Failure	Regrouping, learning, trying again

Words matter. And in general, the goal of reframing is make your words more accurate and realistic. Not to sugar-coat whatever you are describing, or engage in baseless positive thinking, but rather to speak to yourself with the same care and compassion you would use with anyone else you love – and in the process, open more possibilities for handling fearful situations.

Exercise: The Reframing Shop

You work in a framing shop, and love your job framing pictures, photos, and diplomas for people. Except when demanding, controlling customers act like nothing you do is ever good enough. Then you get very anxious.

Normally, you start defending yourself and arguing with these people, and you've learned the hard way that this leads to hard feelings and more anxiety. So now, let's try using reframing on your thoughts - while you reframe the customer's picture!

Take each of these thoughts and use reframing techniques to rewrite them. Have fun!

1. Uh-oh. Here comes Sally. She is always such a control freak.

2. Nothing ever makes her happy.

3. I always freak out around people like her and want to fall through the floor.

4. She'll probably end up going to my boss and getting me fired.

5. If that happens, I'll be out of money, lose my apartment and my car, and I'll probably have to move to a rotten neighborhood.

Developing Agency

Do you know how a doctor gets a nervous child to calm down before giving him a shot? She asks him, "Which arm would you like the shot in?" You see, by giving this child a choice, he feels he has more control, and getting the shot now seems more tolerable.

This is an example of a concept we call *agency*: the ability to take action and have control of a situation. Agency is a core principle of psychotherapy: in general, the more agency you have, the better you feel. Even in a difficult situation. Distress comes from feeling like a helpless victim of circumstance, while confidence builds when you have more of a sense of agency.

Here is a simple two-step process for putting more agency into your own self-talk:

1) Name the situation
2) Complete the phrase, "and I will ..." and add it to the end of the sentence

Let's look at some examples:

Old thought: "I will fail miserably on this test."
New thought: "This will be a difficult test, and I will study hard enough to try and know the answer to at least 80 per cent of the questions on it."

Old thought: "Everyone will be looking at me."
New thought: "Probably one out of 200 people will be looking at me. And I will smile and wave to them if they do."

Old thought: "I was a complete jerk."
New thought: "I responded angrily to something that bothered me. And I will have another conversation with this person soon to clear the air."

Whatever your exact wording, the strategy here is to turn scary feelings and self-critical statements into *skills* and *choices* – and then watch your anxiety go down. The more agency you can legitimately put into your self-talk, the better you will feel. More important, more agency will lead you to effective action towards working with your fears.

Changing Your Mood by Changing Your Thoughts

The vast majority of human distress is caused by the stories that we tell ourselves. More often than not, our fears have their roots in emotionally-charged narratives full of exaggeration and helplessness. Changing the language of these stories is an important first step toward managing our anxiety.

Your goal isn't to completely banish these anxious thoughts. Rather, your goal is to "invite these thoughts to dinner": get to know their legitimate points, learn from them, and make them less scary! Then, you can try on these new thoughts for size -

and then go forward and make small changes in your behavior. These behavioral changes will be what eventually changes most fears, as we will discuss in subsequent chapters.

Finally, changing your thought patterns to be more realistic is more than just a good technique for managing your fears. Over time, and with practice, this type of thinking eventually becomes a way of life – which, in turn, can lower your level of both general and situational anxiety. It is a win-win situation that gets better with practice, and you can start trying it as soon as today!

Today's Action Plan

- Write down your fearful thoughts, and look for *cognitive distortions* – errors in thinking.
- Use *reframing* to change emotional statements to factual ones.
- Create *agency* by rewriting your self-talk around what you will do.

CHAPTER 7

Guided Imagery and Visualization

Did you know that if you practice your tennis serve or your golf swing in your mind first, they will often improve in real life? A quick search of the Internet will reveal numerous articles, books and videos about using your mind to improve your game in many sports.

Visualization – the art of rehearsing something in your mind – is a powerful tool for improving your performance. In many ways, your mind cannot differentiate imagined experience from real life experience. This is a principle you can leverage to get a jump start on working on your fears – by imagining yourself in these situations first. This chapter explores how you can incorporate imagery and visualization into your own personal strategy for overcoming your fears.

Visualization: A Tool You Already Use

If you suffer from anxiety, you already successfully use visualization every day: it's called worry! Worry is nothing more than visualizing a feared outcome over and over in your mind, and reacting emotionally to these mental images. Negative visualization, or worry, is a big part of the reason that people get anxious and stay anxious in specific situations.

This is because your mind cannot easily distinguish between real experience and imagined experience. The things you think about, and focus on, play a major role in your emotions. But you can leverage this same trait to rehearse positive guided imagery that can help you fight your fears.

Visualization - or the ability to picture something in your imagination - can be a useful healing tool for anxiety at two separate levels:

1. Using guided imagery to create a "safe place" in your mind to which you can retreat and refresh yourself.
2. Rehearsing anxious situations in your mind, to practice coping with them or mastering them, before you enter the actual situation.

Let's look at both of these in more detail.

Guided Imagery

Picture a warm, sunny spring day. You are out at a picnic with your best friends. Everyone is having a great time. And now it is time to eat, and you are picking up on the delightful smell of your favorite food cooking on the barbecue. You head over towards the grill, and put some of this delicious food on your plate.

Now, did you just salivate?

If you did, you experienced an example of guided imagery: a piece of experience brought to life through suggestion. As you just experienced, these images create real physiological and emotional reactions. In a very real sense, you were there in the scene that you created.

You can use a similar approach for creating a safe, warm, comfortable space in your mind. A place you can use to ground yourself as you think about anxious situations, and return to over and over. And a place that reminds you of the strong, intelligent, likeable person you really are. Here are some ideas for this safe place:

- Think of a peak experience in your life. For example, achieving a goal, falling in love with someone, or making people proud of you. Connect with how you felt back then, and how the people around you reacted.
- Imagine your favorite place – real or imaginary. Drink it in with all of your senses: sights, sounds, touch, and smell.
- Picture yourself as the hero of your own story, proudly accomplishing things you have always dreamed of doing.
- Take advantage of commercial audio programs that lead you into a deep state of calm and relaxation, in conjunction with the physical relaxation techniques we discussed in Chapter 4.

These mental images can then become a place you start from, and return to, as you imagine conquering your fears in your mind – in small steps, or perhaps with more gusto. We will discuss this in more detail in the next section. Additionally, you can use these images as a pleasant escape from your own negative thought patterns.

For example, when I was being treated for agoraphobia decades ago, I pictured myself on sitting on the lush grass outside of my fraternity in college on a warm spring afternoon, with my friends nearby, my favorite music playing, and not a care in the world. My therapist would have me return to this image over and over, and then switch my attention to mastering a feared situation successfully. It was a simple but effective way to link my efforts with the warmth of my own inner strength and happiness.

Finally, a word to those whose past memories or life experiences may cause a lot of pain. Exercises like these might feel unpleasant or triggering for you – and if this is the case, listen to your gut and please don't force yourself. Consider that guided mental images do not have to be based on real life: you may find that you can rescript a story or mental image where you are happy, triumphant or at peace in ways that you choose to imagine. Either way, trust your best judgment, and know that you can still make progress on the things you fear.

> **Using Imagery for Sweet Dreams**
>
> *Do you suffer from scary or recurrent nightmares? We all experience unpleasant dreams from time to time, but in some cases these dreams are an ongoing problem for some people. In fact, recurrent nightmares are one of the most common symptoms for those who suffer from post-traumatic stress disorder or PTSD.*
>
> *A form of guided imagery known as imagery rehearsal therapy (IRT) has been shown to be clinically effective in reducing the frequency and intensity of these nightmares. Its basic concept is very simple: you take the content of these nightmares, and write a new and more positive script around this content while you are awake.*
>
> *For example, let's say that you frequently dream about being pursued or attacked by someone. Your new script may involve you finding a resourceful way to escape or outsmart this attacker. Better yet, this new script might draw on some of your actual strengths in real life, such as your friends, your communications skills, or your bravery.*

> *IRT has shown a great deal of promise in clinical studies, and I have personally seen very positive results using this strategy with my own clients. It is one more example of how the power of your own mind can actually retrain patterns of negative emotions and help people feel better.*

Rehearsing Anxious Situations

The next chapters of this book will explore what is perhaps the most important part of losing your fears: live practice and gradual exposure. But in many cases, you can use the power of your mind to get a head start on this practice, through imagery desensitization.

This is a similar technique to what the golfers and tennis players we mentioned at the beginning of this chapter do: rehearse a situation in their mind first, so that they practice handling it successfully before attempting it in real life. You pick a gradual step towards the thing you feel – enough to cause you a little anxiety, but not too much – and picture yourself either coping better with it, or even completely triumphing over it. It is your story, with your plot: go ahead and rewrite the script of what happens here! Then you repeat this practice until the thought of this step becomes much less scary.

This technique works best if you can successfully put yourself mentally into this situation, emotionally and physically. You need to feel at least some of the anxiety of the real situation, to practice getting used to it and mastering it in your mind. This means that if you are normally a worrywart, great! Conversely, if you can't feel any anxiety imagining the situation, even though you are uncomfortable with it in real life, this approach will be less useful for you.

Once you have a mental image of the feared situation in mind, hopefully one small step at a time, you can practice being present with this situation, getting used to it, and ultimately mastering it. While practicing, you can either return to the safety of the positive guided imagery we discussed in the previous section as needed, or simply stay with this low-intensity feared situation and work with it. Either way, the goal is to have a safe and productive practice session in your mind.

> **A Structured Process for Visualizing Your Fears**
>
> *Dr. Joseph Strayhorn, the anxiety specialist and author we mentioned in Chapter 5 of this book, uses the acronym STEBC to describe a structured process for imagining yourself coping with or mastering fearful situations:*
>
> **S**ituation: *picture the sights, sounds, and experiences of where you are*
>
> **T**houghts: *imagine what you are thinking in the situation*
>
> **E**motions: *connect with what you are feeling as you succeed*
>
> **B**ehaviors: *visualize how you are acting*
>
> **C**elebration: *picture how you would celebrate after you cope with or master the situation*
>
> *For much more detail on his approach, check out his book A Programmed Course in Anxiety Reduction and Courage Skills (Psychological Skills Press, 2012).*

Imagery desensitization is not for everyone. As we mentioned in the previous section, some people may find trying to experience a fearful situation mentally to be triggering. Others may not be able to really experience the feelings of a situation in their mind — this is one area where children, with their vivid imaginations, are often much better than adults! But for those for whom it works, it has several benefits:

- You can explore fearful situations from within the safety of your own mind
- You can "dose measure" your exposure at any pace you choose
- You can imagine yourself in situations that would not be realistic for live exposure — for example, a fear of confrontation, or a phobia about an unlikely low-probability event
- You can augment live practice sessions, which we discuss in the following chapters, with imagery sessions to increase your total practice time — and hopefully get well quicker

For many people — including me personally, many years ago — guided imagery and visualization can be an important part of learning to face your fears. Now, let's move to the next chapter and learn how to safely and productively address these fears in real life.

Today's Action Plan
- Use guided imagery to create a safe, comfortable place in your mind.
- Use your natural storytelling skills to rewrite the script of fearful situations, and even your nightmares.
- Use imagery desensitization to practice facing your fears in your mind, before you practice with them in real life.

Section IV. Facing Your Fears Successfully

CHAPTER 8

Gradual Exposure: From Thoughts to Action

This chapter's topic is perhaps the most important one of all: how to start making the behavioral changes that help you permanently erase your irrational fears.

First, let's recap what we've learned in the previous chapters, and how it all leads to making changes in your behavior:

- First, we learned about how and why we get anxious - and that we all *choose* to be anxious, at some level, because of what we tell ourselves. This doesn't mean that we are stupid - and it doesn't mean that we can just snap our fingers and stop being anxious! But it does mean that anxiety doesn't just "happen" to us. More important, we can change it using specific, step-by-step techniques.
- We then learned how to be mindfully aware of our anxious thoughts and feelings, ground ourselves in our senses, and make wise choices as a compassionate observer.

- Next, we learned some powerful physical techniques for controlling our anxiety, such as breathing, progressive muscle relaxation and autogenic relaxation.
- Then we learned how to identify common errors in what we think - and how to use powerful techniques to identify what we are really telling ourselves when we are anxious, and change these anxious thoughts to realistic ones.

So how do you feel after doing all of these things? Probably a little better, but still anxious, right?

Here is why you still feel that way: you must change your *behavior* to change your anxiety. For exactly the same reason you become a better golfer by hitting the links, not just thinking about your game. Learning new behaviors become habits - and these habits are what ultimately erase your fears. Which leads us to a very powerful concept that, for many if not most people, will be the key to getting better.

The Key to Losing Your Fears: Playing the Short Game

When you learned to ride a bicycle for the first time, did your parents take off the training wheels, push you out into the middle of heavy traffic, and tell you to "sink or swim"?

Ironically, that is what many of us do when we try to change our anxiety behaviors. We use the "Nike approach" - just do it. And then we wonder why we don't get any better.

Under some circumstances, Nike therapy actually could work: if you stick with a fearful situation long enough to get used to it, your fear can be reduced for the future. We call this process *habituation*. Under the guidance of a therapist, there is nothing wrong with this kind of sustained exposure.

The problem is that many people can't – or won't – stick with a fearful situation long enough to habituate to it. So their bravery actually works against them. What happens is they summon their bravery, get themselves into the fearful situation, discover they are too uncomfortable, and retreat back to safety. And that safety feels so good, it reinforces the idea of running away from the things they fear – with the result that they feel more stuck than ever in the future!

This is why we propose a different approach: one that is easier, gentler, but still very effective. Here is its mantra:

Start in your comfort zone, stay in your comfort zone, and see where you can take your comfort zone from week to week.

In other words, do what you can every day to challenge your boundaries and face what you are afraid of – but do it in small, comfortable steps. And see where these steps take you as you practice from day to day.

I call this *playing the short game*. It is a sports analogy: it means that instead of worrying about the whole game, you focus your attention on what you are doing at this moment – for example, during this at-bat in baseball, or this serve in tennis. The focus changes from long-term strategy to short-term execution. When it comes to your anxiety, it means that your only job – and your only concern – is the next small step.

This also means that you don't shame yourself for where you are at right now. That would be like expecting to play at Carnegie Hall after your first trumpet lesson. The emotional and spiritual goal of playing the short game is to commit to a process of gradual change, and look for small gains relative to where you are at now. This is important because even when you start making progress, we all have a natural tendency to discount our gains. ("I can now go further from the house than ever. But I can still only go half a mile away.") Your first steps toward your fears will seem positively lame. Accept and embrace this lame-ness, because you are on a trajectory to wellness.

Are you thinking that you play the short game already? No, you probably aren't. Instead, you probably either avoid fearful situations entirely, or hurl yourself at these situations every so often and freak yourself out. You probably aren't nibbling away at these fears in a planned, systematic way. But this is precisely where learning best takes place, and how many people finally lose their fears.

Playing the short game has two critical components:

1. Regular practice. Ideally, I would like to see you spend an hour per day, at least five days per week, testing your boundaries and seeing what you can comfortably do each day. Clinically, I feel that the act of practicing is even more important than how *intensely* you practice. And the reason that most people stay stuck with their fears isn't that they aren't brave enough: it is that they aren't getting enough "reps" (repetition cycles, in exercise parlance).

2. Being fully present. This is the other critical component to losing your fears. Right now, when you get into a fearful situation, you probably shut down or distract yourself. You pop a Valium, crank up the music, text your best friend, or try to tune out those painful feelings of anxiety. *No learning takes place when you do any of these things*, so the next time, you are no less anxious. Instead, I want you to be fully present in the situation: take in the sights, sounds, and feelings of where you are. Connect with the fact that you are warm, safe, dry – and *here*.

This is where taking small steps comes in. When the steps are small enough, you are comfortable practicing every day, and comfortable being fully present in the situation as you practice. This is the zone where learning takes place, and your boundaries start to expand. And in the end, losing your fears becomes lots and lots of easy. Now let's look at a strategy for making this happen.

Creating a Hierarchy

Most anxiety behaviors are easier to change when you attack them step-by-step - which means the first step is often creating a hierarchy with lots of gradual steps, from least anxious to most anxious. This hierarchy then becomes your personal plan for attacking your fears.

A hierarchy works hand-in-hand with the "new" scripts you create for your anxious thoughts, by allowing you to test out these new thoughts with new behaviors. This is how your anxiety starts to go away.

Some fears naturally lend themselves to a hierarchy - for example, when someone is afraid to leave home, you can measure how many steps you are from home. At one end of the hierarchy, you take a half-step outside the door - and at the other end, you might be boarding a flight to Chicago. Other fears might be more complicated. For example, someone with complex OCD rituals might be able to make small changes to make them less demanding - or delay performing them - or start eliminating them a piece at a time.

A good hierarchy should have a list of behaviors combined with a rating (say, from 1 to 100) of how anxious these behaviors normally make you. Zero is no anxiety at all, and 100 is the worst anxiety you could possibly imagine: something that might land you in the hospital, for example. This scale is known as your Subjective Units of Discomfort, or SUDS for short. Here is one possible example of a hierarchy for someone who has social anxiety disorder:

Action	Anxiety level (SUDS)
Spend two hours at a crowded party where you will be the center of everyone's attention - on a boat where you cannot leave.	100
Go grocery shopping at high noon on Saturday in a store crowded with people.	70
Go to a baseball game where classmates might come over and say hello.	50
Walk outside in your garden when your next-door neighbor might wave at you.	30
Go to the mailbox and get the mail at midday with cars going by.	25
Go to the mailbox and get the mail late at night.	15
Step on your front porch for 30 seconds and then step back in.	10

The more steps you have at the lower rungs of the hierarchy - and the less anxiety they cause you - the better. These "baby steps" give you small steps that let you try new behaviors as you change the script of what you tell yourself.

Exercise: A Hierarchy for Archie

Archie is an OCD sufferer who has developed a complex ritual that involves about 14 steps - before he can leave his room, he has to touch the door, touch himself, pray, step from side to side, and so forth. If he doesn't do this, it feels like "bad luck" and he worries about it.

When Archie doesn't do all the steps correctly, which is often, he has to do the whole ritual over - so it isn't unusual for it to take

> him an hour to get out of his room in the morning, and he often feels exhausted and depressed.
>
> Let's say that for Archie, doing his favorite activity of sitting in bed watching Saturday morning cartoons has zero anxiety for him, and leaving his room immediately without doing the ritual would be close to 100 on the anxiety scale.
>
> - *What "baby steps" might he take at first?*
>
> - *What bigger steps might be longer-term goals?*
>
> - *What if he can't come up with a good hierarchy about the rituals at first - it feels like "all or nothing." What else might he work on? (Hint: he can vary things like how much time he spends, or how well he performs the ritual.)*

Now, what if your fear doesn't lend itself well to a hierarchy? Here are some examples:

- You are afraid of taking a long plane flight. (Once you're on the plane, you're on it)
- You dread having a family member get angry at you. (You aren't exactly going to provoke a fight for the sake of practice)
- You are uncomfortable driving in bad weather. (And lately it has been sunny for the past two weeks.)
- You are worried about a low-probability event such as a zombie invasion. (You've been watching too much television. And it's hard to find zombies to practice on.)

All is not lost here. First, you have the option of practicing imagery desensitization, as we discussed in the previous chapter. Second, you can use cognitive restructuring to change the way you think about these scary situations. Third, you can keep practicing mindful awareness and physical relaxation skills to learn how to cope better.

But more often than not, you can still create a behavioral hierarchy and get some live practice toward these situations. How? By breaking them down into their component parts, looking for transferable or analogous situations to these component parts, and practicing on them. Let's take a fresh look at these situations again:

Situation	Practice Strategy
Long plane flight	Spend time in a small space, or take a bus trip
Angry family member	Role-play angry situations with a good friend, and learn how to communicate assertively in them
Driving in bad weather	Practice defensive driving strategies in a deserted parking lot
Zombie invasion	Watch a television show or movie about zombies, alone or with a friend, and strategize how you would survive

The more fun you can make an exposure, the better. For example, don't just practice eating in a restaurant – have your all-time favorite meal somewhere. Or whistle your favorite tune as you practice being out in public. Whatever helps you feel better AND be fully present with the situation can become part of your practice repertoire.

Finally, if your fears involve intrusive thoughts, as we discussed in a previous chapter, your initial exposure is to *the thought itself* – let it come and go, and learn that it is just a thought. Your goal is to gradually learn to ignore these thoughts. In time, this kind of practice will lessen their intensity, just like any fear.

Exposure: Working with Your Hierarchy

Now, here comes the fun part: starting to change your behavior. There are three "levels" of exposing yourself to your fears:

1. Flooding. This is "Nike therapy" - you simply do whatever you are most afraid of, no matter how anxious you feel, and don't give in to your fears. Flooding is not commonly used - it can work in some cases (with a long enough exposure), but may in fact sensitize you to your fears rather than desensitize you to them. Fun fact: when one recent study measured the effectiveness of flooding on people with anxiety disorders, they had to stop the study because everyone quit!
Example: You are afraid of riding in elevators, so you decide to take an elevator to the top of the Empire State Building.

2. Sustained exposure. Here, you choose an activity that isn't comfortable, but isn't overwhelming either. You commit to exposing yourself to it, and stick with it until your anxiety level goes down – in clinical terms, you "habituate" or get used to the stimulus.
Example: Riding on an elevator makes you anxious, at about a 25 out of 100 level. You keep riding up and down the elevators for an hour until you start feeling better.

3. Gradual exposure. This is the approach we are proposing in this book. Instead of getting anxious and getting used to a situation, you stay relatively comfortable and gradually expand your comfort zone. The pros of this approach is that it is easier to do – the cons are that it takes longer and requires more "baby steps."

Example: First you simply step in and out of an elevator. Then you close the doors and then open them immediately. Then you take the elevator one floor at a time until you are completely comfortable. Then two floors. Then three. Eventually get to where you can hang around in elevators with no problem.

If you think about it, there are probably things that you can do, without even breaking a sweat, that move your boundaries a little further along for most fears:

- Afraid to leave the house? Take a few steps from home – and if you are feeling too anxious, stop.
- Uncomfortable starting conversations with people? Smile or say hello at the checkout clerk at the store.
- Afraid of spiders? Look briefly at a picture of one.
- Fear confrontation with your boss? Ask her for a very small favor.
- Wash your hands compulsively? Spend a few less seconds doing it each time.

And what if these steps are still too much? No problem – make them even smaller. The key here is to do whatever is possible in the moment, and keep exploring what is possible in the future.

> **The Blood Test Analogy**
>
> *When I am creating a hierarchy with a client in a therapy session, I often start by asking them if they are afraid to have their blood drawn at the doctor's office. Some adults are, in fact, uncomfortable with this, but most are not.*

> *I go on to explain that I am not afraid to have my blood drawn either – I don't lay awake at night worrying about it the night before, I don't even really think about it driving to the doctor's, and I wouldn't dream of running away at the last minute and skipping it. But the way I feel just as they are about to jab the needle in my arm – let's call that a five on an anxiety scale of zero to 100 – that is the zone where I want most people to practice exposing themselves to their fears. I want them to pick something no scarier than my blood draw to work on each day.*
>
> *So what if a client is afraid to have their blood drawn? No problem – we find another metaphor that makes sense for them. But the goal is to have exposure therapy feel liberating, not frightening.*

From here, the goal is to take things one step at a time until you learn to be less anxious in that situation, before moving on to the next step. For example, if something is a five on your SUDS scale, get it to where it is close to zero – and positively boring, rather than anxiety-provoking – before you move on. And whatever anxiety level you start practicing at, be sure to get your level to at least five or less.

Also, be prepared for your SUDS level to vary from day to day. One day you feel great and can go a couple of steps up the hierarchy, the next day you can't comfortably do anywhere near as much. This is OK and completely normal. *Just do whatever you can that day, and worry about tomorrow tomorrow*. Each day's results are not particularly important: what is important is their trend over time.

This strategy of combining small steps with regular practice is similar to what many great athletes and performers do to hone their skills. For example, have you ever watched Nik Wallenda, the tightrope walker who has crossed the Grand Canyon and ridden a bicycle on a wire over Niagara Falls? He practices his acts over and over on a wire just a few feet off the ground, with wind machines simulating the weather conditions. In other words, *he keeps himself safe and comfortable at all times, which in turn allows him to do lots and lots of practice.* A similar strategy can be the key to losing your fears too.

> **Important Disclaimer**
>
> *If you are seeking therapy for your anxiety disorders independent of reading this book, your therapist may be using a different approach to exposure therapy than we propose here. They may feel you are capable of handling a stronger level of exposure – or that you aren't ready to do any exposure at all. That is because they know how to evaluate and treat you personally, while this book is written for a general audience of readers.*
>
> *A core concept of this book is to attack your fears in small, comfortable steps. But always consult with your own therapist for how to proceed with your own specific treatment, and follow their personalized advice first.*

Your Goal: Keep Following the Steps

Ultimately, the goal of gradual exposure therapy is to lose your fears. So how long will it take? This is a trick question.

If you divide your goal into 100 steps, you might think the answer is 100 steps. But usually it isn't. It may be fourteen, or seven, or twenty. But at some point, if you keep practicing, a switch will flip inside your brain. More often than you might think, your amygdala will decide that something isn't as scary as it used to be, and the fear will fail catastrophically.

This was how I personally recovered from severe agoraphobia decades ago. My therapist had me drive on an unfamiliar road, a quarter of a mile at a time, with my wife following me in her car. My orders were to turn back as soon as I felt uncomfortable, and NOT press on any further. At first, it seemed really lame. I could go a quarter of a mile down the road, then a half mile, then three quarters of a mile – big whoop.

But then one week, one mile turned into two. And then five. And then it was, "Honey, let's try driving an hour away to Syracuse and go shopping." And before long, to my amazement, I was making airline reservations to visit my parents, who had recently moved clear across the US to Arizona. By the time I returned from that trip – which went surprisingly well – I was free.

Your mileage may vary, literally and figuratively. But I see the same thing over and over nowadays as a therapist treating other people: regular, steady practice eventually crumbles many of the things people fear, such as:

- Being afraid to leave the safety of home
- Feeling like you have to obey a compulsive ritual like checking or washing your hands.
- Fearing situations like turbulence on an airplane.
- Being uncomfortable in social situations or interviews.
- Not knowing how to respond to criticism.

One letter I received from a patient who struggled with a fear of heights – and practiced gradual exposure, one small step at a time – perhaps sums it up best:

"Put me in the WIN column! I am writing this email from our condo on vacation. Let me be more specific... from the outdoor balcony of our TWELFTH FLOOR condo! Yesterday I rode a roller coaster. A ROLLER - FREAKING COASTER!!!! I was stuck high up in the air... by myself... for the whole ride. I was a little apprehensive, but I DID NOT PANIC!!!!!

While before I was terrified to live and terrified to die, I am now excited to live! All because of your teaching and support, and really because somehow you were able to convince me it's possible. Thank you, thank you, thank you. Use me in your case studies, books, in talking to your patients. I know it's a lifetime journey, but I'm finally on it."

Today's Action Plan

- Break your fears down into small steps if possible, and create a hierarchy that you can use to practice gradual exposure.
- Practice expanding your boundaries – in safe, gradual steps – for at least one hour per day, five days per week.
- Make it a point to be fully present when you are practicing, and do not distract yourself.

CHAPTER 9

Handling Unplanned "Life Exposures"

Let's say that you are cruising along making progress on a fear of leaving home. Last week you were comfortable a few steps from home, and now you can go as far as three blocks without fear. But now you've got a toothache and need to go to the dentist, who is five miles away!

Situations like these are what we call "life exposures": situations that are outside of your comfort zone, that you have to do. Some of these may include:

- Important family obligations such as weddings, funerals, or reunions.
- School or work obligations.
- Health issues that require treatment.
- Personal obligations such as jury duty or court appearances.
- Things you want that require you to stretch: for example, you are offered a dream job on the 20th floor when you have elevator fears, or a great date with someone when you have social fears.

Life exposures can be transformational experiences, or they can be setbacks. Most often, they are neither: they are simply experiences to be endured and moved past, like a root canal. And the skills you use for dealing with them are not the same as your long-term plan for losing these fears.

It is important to understand that these life exposures are fundamentally different from exposure therapy for your fears: while some therapists may prescribe strong exposures as a therapeutic tool, to help people "habituate" or get used to the situation, so-called "life exposures" generally fall outside of these planned, therapeutic experiences. The good news, however, is that they can be understood and managed with a few specific tools.

Dealing with "Life Exposures"

The first thing to understand about life exposures is that they are fundamentally different than practicing losing your fears. Therefore, they often require a different strategy for handling them.

You see, with normal practice, your job is to learn to be fully present with small doses of a feared situation. In a life exposure, by comparison, your goal is to live to fight another day. To do what you have to do, and get through it without getting too uncomfortable.

This doesn't mean that you can't learn something from life exposures. Sometimes they may even be transformational – knowing that you made it through a very uncomfortable situation can build your confidence for the future. And sometimes, sticking out a bad situation long enough can lead some people to "habituate" or get used to it. But it is equally important to learn tools and skills for managing situations that are far outside of your normal comfort zone. Here are some of the key ones:

Have plenty of "outs." As paradoxical as it sounds, you will feel stronger going into a situation if you know what you can do to escape, endure, or feel better. Some examples of "outs" include:

- Knowing you can find a quiet place to hide if you have social anxiety.
- Knowing there are earlier flights home if you have travel anxiety.
- Knowing you can take an extended "bathroom break" if you get too anxious.

The purpose of a good out is not to avoid a situation, but rather to strengthen you to go *into* a situation. They work best with a mindset that using an out when needed is good judgment — because paradoxically, being too reluctant to use an out won't make it seem like a good out in the first place. The key is to feel more comfortable knowing that you have these outs in your back pocket.

> *Exercise: Strike Three, Your "Outs"*
>
> *Casey has long dreamed of being a professional baseball pitcher. And now, after years of toiling in the minors, he has been called up to start for a major league team this weekend. So how does Casey feel? Petrified!*
>
> *You see, Casey suffers from social anxiety disorder. And the thought of having 50,000 fans hanging on every pitch when he starts against the Cubs this weekend has him terrified. Not to mention that his whole family, who are proud of his baseball*

> *career - and always dismissed his "crazy" anxiety concerns - will be in the stands.*
>
> - *What kinds of "outs" might you suggest for Casey? Hint: think of big ones and little ones.*
>
> - *Baseball pitchers are famous for having their own pre-game rituals. What might you suggest for Casey?*
>
> - *What errors in thinking might be making Casey feel even worse?[3]*

Be driven to distraction. Normally, in exposure therapy, distraction is a bad thing - your goal is to be present in the situation and learn to be comfortable. But with a "life exposure," distraction can be an important way to get through the situation.

Distraction techniques can be social, physical, or even medical. Talk with people, listen to music, write, or compose your next sonata! Or lean on temporary medications, in consultation with your prescriber or physician, to help you feel more comfortable.

Just be aware that distraction is generally not a good strategy for practicing gradual exposure to your fears. The reason most of us try - and fail - to become less anxious about situations by "gutting them out" is that we instinctively distract ourselves during them, and never learn to be present and comfortable in them. But in a life exposure, these same tools can help you get through it.

---

[3] This scenario is not as farfetched as it sounds. One of the most dominant major league pitchers of the 21st century, Cy Young Award winner Zach Greinke, has suffered from severe social anxiety disorder and at one point walked away from the game in 2006. Source: http://en.wikipedia.org/wiki/Zach_Greinke

Get out of your thoughts and into your senses. We discussed this strategy earlier, as part of our chapter on developing mindful awareness. In the middle of a "life exposure," you want to ground yourself in your physical environment. Whether it is people-watching, feeling the wind on your face, or smelling the rich aromas of good food, engaging your senses is a powerful antidote to anxiety. And the more senses you can use – sight, sound, touch, hearing – the better.

Grounding yourself in your physical reality has two important benefits in an anxious situation. First, you are short-circuiting the racing thoughts that keep fueling your anxiety, by giving you something else to focus your mind's limited short-term attention on. Second, you stay in the moment: a moment where things are OK, here and now, and will probably be OK in the next moment as well.

Take care of yourself. This is the classic response of every pop psychology article about stress: get enough sleep, eat right, take a bubble bath, etc.

We often tend to ignore this advice because these things often don't take the anxiety away. And you are correct: they don't. But self-care rituals are, in fact, very important for giving yourself the strength you need for handling a "life exposure," for two reasons: (a) they help you feel better and less "out of control" physically, and (b) they help you affirm your self-worth in the face of the situation.

> *What Emotionally Unstable People Do Better Than You*
>
> *When I describe someone as emotionally unstable, it isn't an insult. It is a clinical description, just like having brown hair or wearing glasses. So I mean it in the nicest possible way.*

This is because emotionally unstable personality disorder, also known as borderline personality disorder or BPD, is an actual diagnosis. And it is often quite treatable for many people who suffer from it. Which brings me to the topic at hand – emotionally unstable people who are successfully treated do something that would also benefit each and every one of us, if we did it. **They learn to behave counterintuitively in their worst moments.**

For example, a BPD sufferer and his partner may agree that when he is having a "borderline moment" and acting agitated, that he will take a break and continue the conversation later – or perhaps binge-watch his favorite TV show first. The key is that they agree ahead of time to execute a plan, one which may in fact go against his human nature, because it works for them.

The same thing is true for people with fears and phobias. Instead of ruminating about these situations, it may make more sense to watch a ballgame first. Or engage in some self-soothing behavior. Or team up with a friend for support. Whatever helps you get in to the situation, and get through the situation.

So take a tip from emotionally unstable people: acting on your feelings is not always a good idea, and making an alternative plan of action in advance is often the key to peace of mind. Because as Benjamin Franklin once said, those who fail to plan often plan to fail.

To sum it all up: Exposure therapy involves gradual, purposeful exposures designed to change the way you think about an anxious situation. "Life exposures," by comparison, are challenges that may fall far beyond these boundaries. The good news is that with self-care, distraction, and proper "escape planning," you can manage these situations and get through them as well.

Today's Action Plan

- Develop good "outs" that you can use in a scary situation in the future, to give yourself more of a sense of control.
- Think of how you might distract yourself in these situations.
- Come up with good self-care strategies to soothe yourself in a difficult situation.

CHAPTER 10

Setbacks, Stuck Points and Coaching

This chapter wraps up our section on exposure therapy by discussing three of the most common areas people have questions about: experiencing setbacks, feeling "stuck" in their exposure strategy, and how best to coach and support anxiety sufferers in their family.

Dealing with Setbacks

It happens sometimes. Your exposure practice is going along fine, and then something really freaks you out. And then you feel like you are back to square one again.

Except you aren't. Setbacks are a normal occurrence during exposure therapy. Why? Because you are human. We don't feel the same from day to day, circumstances vary, and it is completely normal to bravely face something one day and want to run screaming from it the next. But it is still a very upsetting experience to feel like you are losing ground.

Here are some things to do when you experience a setback:

Explore what is happening in your life. Sometimes a setback reflects events or feelings that are going on outside of your exposure practice. If you've just experienced news of a life change (good or bad), or had a run-in with your boss, or had too many cups of coffee, it may make sense for things to have gone differently today.

The same is true for your overall physical sense of well-being, because mind and body are often closely linked. For example, one hot summer evening I was at a hotel in Phoenix, visiting my family on vacation, when I noticed that I was feeling very depressed. This was unusual for me, because I rarely get depressed without a clear reason. As the night wore on, I also realized that I wasn't feeling well physically, and when I took my temperature late that evening, I was running a 102 degree fever. So I wasn't depressed after all – I was sick! Once I understood what was happening, my feelings didn't seem strange at all, and I knew I simply had to rest.

Cultivate acceptance. Having a setback is scary. And I would not ask you to pretend that it is anything other than scary. But I would not want you to add to that burden by criticizing yourself, calling yourself a failure, or worrying about how things will go tomorrow.

The fact is that setbacks are normal, and the only rational way to describe them is as something you should expect and work with. The fact that you had a setback is a sign that you are still actively in the process of losing your fears – just like a bad play on the football field means you are still in the game. So go ahead and tell yourself it was unpleasant, or no fun, but then let tomorrow be tomorrow – and get back in the saddle and practice again.

Keep playing the short game. If there is one most important principle for recovering from a setback, it is to keep practicing.

The same principle applies after a setback: don't worry about how much you can do, but whatever you can do, keep doing it. Be willing to have good days and bad days, and continue to work the process itself.

At the end of the day, it isn't expected — nor is it even particularly important — to always be on a continual upward trajectory. What is important is keeping your perspective, and continuing to use the tools and skills you have learned. This is ultimately how you will make progress in losing your fears.

Getting Past Stuck Points

Actual practice with a hierarchy, if you take small enough steps, can be surprisingly comfortable - in fact, getting well from anxiety disorders is often easier than continuing to suffer with your symptoms! But what about those situations where you feel "stuck"? Here are some common reasons for this:

Your steps are too big. Ideally, using this approach, you should be practicing with situations that normally are less than a 10 or at most 20 on the SUDS scale - minor twinges, not major anxieties. Your goal here is to start comfortable, stay comfortable, and gradually expand your comfort zone.

You haven't done your homework. Don't just blindly start doing exposures - first, use the cognitive techniques we have discussed previously to identify your core thoughts, rewrite those thoughts to be more rational, and then do the exposure.

You have too many outside stresses. No one's life is ever completely free of stress, but situations like major life changes, loss, or trauma are often less than ideal for trying to do exposure therapy.

It may be time to try something else. If all else fails, perhaps this approach may not work for your situation right now. Even the best evidence-based approaches are not 100% effective. Give gradual exposure a fair trial (as long as it does not conflict with your individual therapy), and then explore other options.

On this last point, understand that human beings – and their situations – can vary a great deal. One person may be recovering from a trauma, and may benefit from consulting a trauma-focused therapist before attempting exposure therapy. Another may have an undiagnosed physical problem, such as diabetes or thyroid problems, affecting their anxiety level. Still another may have a drug or alcohol issue that might be interfering with their self-help efforts. You deserve to have the best care you can find, including consulting with specialists and getting second opinions where needed.

That said, for most people gradual exposure therapy is generally very effective, if you keep trying and give it time. Let's put some numbers to this, based on my own practice having treated several hundred anxiety sufferers. Out of every 10 people who consult me about treatment for fears and phobias:

- Probably seven or so will lose their fears or function a great deal better, using standard cognitive-behavioral therapy and gradual exposure (the approach we discuss in this book).
- One or two people will feel this approach doesn't work for them. And they are probably right – there may be issues ranging from unprocessed trauma to other co-existing conditions that get in the way. Or perhaps it simply doesn't make enough sense to them to try it.

- Another one or two people will receive the message of exposure therapy with great joy, but then disappear from therapy before actually doing any exposures, never to be seen again. I feel they are right too – they realize they aren't ready to do this yet. And hopefully we have planted some seeds for a time when they may feel more ready in the future.

This success rate – about 70 percent or so – is consistent with what I see in the literature. More important, it represents a vast improvement in success rates over the space of just a few decades. So keep educated, and stay optimistic: if you are like most people, you can achieve significant relief from your fears.

> *Exercise: Building Trust*
>
> *Velma is afraid to go grocery shopping by herself. When she was a little girl, she was once threatened by bullies near the produce aisle, when her mother wasn't looking.*
>
> *But now Velma is 47 years old, and friends and relatives are tired of doing her shopping for her. Think about how you might answer the following questions:*
>
> - *How could you start building up Velma's trust that she is safe in a grocery store?*
>
> - *What kinds of "behavioral experiments" might you suggest Velma try to help her feel safer?*
>
> - *What kinds of cognitive distortions (e.g. errors in thinking) might be going on with Velma? How might she use these cognitive distortions to feel better about going to the store?*

Coaching the Right Way: Advice for Families and Partners

And now, a word to parents, partners and other family members who live with an anxiety sufferer. I mean this in the nicest possible way: you are probably coaching them wrong.

The reason is human nature. Parenting, for example, is often about "tough love", or coaching children to do things they don't want to do. And there is a point to it: If it wasn't for at least some tough love, many of us would have never gone to school, learned how to tie our shoes, or figured out how to control our behavior. We would all be eating ice cream five times a day and sleeping until noon.

Partners often have a similar "coaching" relationship with each other - whether it is helping the other person succeed, or getting them to pick up around the house, we often try to influence the people close to us.

So it often seems natural for parents or other family members to bring the same kind of "tough love" approach to anxiety treatment. Unfortunately this approach can work against you, for a number of reasons:

- Effective exposure often comes in comfortable baby steps. When a parent or partner sets goals or over-monitors progress, the anxious person often tries to do too much, to please you or avoid judgment - which can sensitize rather than desensitize their anxieties.
- When a parent or partner sets an anxiety goal, rather than the anxious person, these goals often become "life exposures" that are endured rather than experienced differently, as we discussed in the previous chapter.
- Small gains are really important, particularly in the early stages of anxiety treatment. In fact, it is more important to have small steps that are really successful than to have

larger ones that are uncomfortable. When a parent or partner is over-involved, it can minimize the importance of achieving small successes.

In general, exposure therapy works best when it is driven by the anxiety sufferer him or herself. But this does not mean that you must remain completely mute – in fact, to the contrary, the right kinds of encouragement and support can be extremely important for successful exposure therapy. However, the key here is that collaboration is good, while expectations and pressure are not.

Let's break this down into statements that help, and statements that don't. First, here are some things that are usually OK to ask an anxiety sufferer:

- How are things going for you?
- What kinds of things have you felt best about in this process?
- Is there anything you feel "stuck" about?
- Can I do anything to help you?

Statements like these "check in" with a sufferer, without taking control of their exposure process or setting expectations for them. By comparison, here are some examples of things that are usually best NOT to ask:

- What exposures did you do today?
- How successful were you?
- What is your goal for today?
- Could you do more? Why haven't you made more progress?

The problem with statements like these is that they implicitly or explicitly set expectations for the sufferer. What's wrong with that, you might ask? The answer is that in addition to seeing how well they can face their fears, the sufferer now has an additional challenge — what you will think of them. This can lead the sufferer to one of two bad outcomes: trying to do more than they are really comfortable with to please you, or becoming disheartened and giving up entirely.

This doesn't mean that you can't talk about concerns you might have about accommodating an anxiety sufferer — for example, if they expect you to do all of their shopping for them, or have compulsive rituals that interfere with the family. We'll discuss that in the next session. Just remember that issues like these are YOUR agenda. When it comes to the sufferer's agenda, the more they can control the process, the better.

In the case of adolescent children in particular, exposure therapy for anxiety is an excellent chance to them to start making adult decisions to benefit themselves. Of course, be sure to compliment any successes that they share with you! And for people of any age, positive encouragement and support is a very important success factor in fighting their fears.

> **Exercise: Motivating Your Sweetie**
>
> *Your spouse has long been anxious about going to work. He worried about being judged, and was traumatized by a confrontation with a toxic boss many years ago.*
>
> *Nowadays he sits in front of the television watching soap operas listlessly, while you are exhausted from your job and struggling to make ends meet. You would love to see him get back to work.*
>
> *What might be the best way to have a productive dialogue with your spouse about constructive ways to get back to work, without putting him on the defensive?*

Negotiating Boundaries

If you are a family member of someone who suffers from anxiety, you also carry a special burden. In an ideal world, you would be supportive and healing when a member of your family suffers from any issue - emotional or physical. In reality, however, an anxiety disorder can be extremely disruptive for everyone in a family:

- Anxiety symptoms appear to be behavioral, not physical, and are often mistaken for laziness, defiance, or passive aggression
- The anxiety sufferer may demand accommodation from the family
- Conversely, anxiety sufferers often do not receive the empathy or support someone with a physical illness receives. People often talk about how "bravely" people deal with physical illnesses, but rarely mental or neurological ones
- Anxiety disorders often challenge people's normal boundaries as a parent, relative or partner

Here are some guidelines for negotiating boundaries that are fair to both sides:

1. Involve the sufferer in the process of deciding these boundaries, including what to accommodate, what responsibilities this person has, and how other people should treat him/her.
2. Be curious, not furious, and take a learning stance based on asking questions rather than criticizing the sufferer.
3. Be flexible, and plan ahead for bad days as well as good days. For example, someone with agoraphobia may need a "get out

of jail free card" that lets them stay home on a particularly bad day, even if they normally leave the house most of the time.

4. Notice and praise small gains, understand and discuss setbacks openly and honestly, and resist the temptation to pressure sufferers to be "normal" too quickly.

5. Once boundaries have been established, create a no-criticism zone around the sufferer's anxiety issues - just like any physical illness.

Consider involving a trained therapist in this dialogue if possible, preferably sooner rather than later. (An analogy: if your child wanted to stay home from school, saying she had a toothache, you might accommodate it - but then the next stop would be the dentist. Similarly, when anxiety becomes a constraint for someone, leverage this to get the sufferer and the family involved in effective treatment.)

Finally, remember that an anxiety sufferer remains a full-fledged member of your household, with the same rights and decision-making privileges as everyone else. Actively seek ways to relate to them in ways that recognize their strengths and talents, and find ways to "need" them as well as just criticize or "help" them. Instead of fostering a dynamic between a sick person and a well person, build a partnership of equals that serves both of you well.

> ***Exercise: Doing the Yard Work***
>
> *Your young daughter has always been fairly sensitive. But lately things have been harder for her, and this week she declared that she wasn't comfortable going outside and doing yard work anymore. When you try to ask her about it, all she can really tell you is that it makes her really uncomfortable. Answer the following questions:*

1) What would you say to her as a parent?

2) Her two older brothers feel that she is getting away with not doing as many chores as they do, and are pretty upset about it. What would you tell them?

3) What do you feel her responsibilities are in the household?

Bonus question: What would you say differently if she was diagnosed with a sprained ankle instead of an anxiety disorder?

Today's Action Plan

- Accept occasional setbacks as a normal part of gradual exposure, and continue practicing.
- If you are feeling "stuck," consider smaller steps, more preparation, or another approach.
- If you are a family member of an anxiety sufferer, learn to communicate effectively about coaching and boundary-setting.

Section V. The Advanced Course

CHAPTER 11

Handling Social Fears

Social anxiety is far and away the most prevalent anxiety disorder. If you look at its numbers, it is also a widespread issue for society. Nearly 15 percent of people suffer from it, while fully a quarter of us are introverts – people who are drained by social interaction, and hate having to "perform" for other people on command. I often tell social anxiety sufferers that they do not have a disorder: they have a perfectly normal way of being, in a society that is simply wired differently.

For extroverts, conversation often feels as natural as breathing. You talk, they talk, and when the conversation reaches a natural stopping point, you bring the dialogue in for a soft landing and take your leave. They truly think by talking, and cannot imagine anyone feeling differently.

For introverts, on the other hand, conversations feel like being on stage with a 300 watt spotlight shining on them. They feel exposed, vulnerable, and embarrassed. They worry that they won't know what to say, and that it will make them look bad. As a result, they avoid situations where they might have to speak with someone — even, sometimes, to the point of refusing to leave their homes.

It is also important to understand that being an introvert – or having social anxiety – does not automatically imply that you are outwardly "shy." Many affable, articulate and seemingly outgoing people are introverts. And social anxiety is a matter of how you feel, rather than how you have learned to act. So rest assured, if you are socially adept but still find situations with people uncomfortable, this is extremely normal.

These feelings are more treatable than you might think. By learning specific, procedural skills, conversations can become predictable and fearless for anyone. Let's look at the mechanics of a normal conversation, and how you can learn to master them.

Why Conversations Seem Frightening

If you are an introvert by nature — or if you have become traumatized by the idea of being in conversation — the desire to be invisible in conversation is often part of your normal human nature. But it also represents an error in thinking.

First of all, introverts fundamentally like to think before they speak. Unlike the 75% of us who are extroverts, and therefore think by talking out loud, the introverted minority wants to be prepared ahead of time about what to say. So the idea of being forced to talk without a complete, fully formed thought can seem painful and uncomfortable. Similarly, introverts often feel drained by human interaction, and try to conserve this precious resource of personal energy.

Now here is where the error in thinking comes in. You probably see a conversation as being more like an improvised musical performance. You are up on stage, you have to rapidly make up the notes as you go along, and you are hanging on for dear life to keep up. And if you hit a single wrong note, everyone notices!

In reality, conversations are more like following a recipe from a cookbook. It is a thoughtfully composed performance that follows a clear structure, using skills that anyone can learn. Once you learn these skills, you can handle any conversation well. To help you do this, let's introduce the *Conversation Worksheet*: a powerful tool that lets you prepare the key ingredients for having a comfortable, fulfilling 5-7 minute conversation with anyone, anytime.

The Conversation Worksheet

1. List 3-5 prepared conversation starters:

_____

_____

_____

2. List the three most likely things for the person you are conversing with to say in response, and how you will acknowledge these:

_____

_____

_____

3. List three questions you can ask the other person:

_____

_____

_____

4. List 3-5 things you can say about yourself:

_____

_____

_____

> 5. List 3-5 prepared "closing phrases" to gracefully exit a conversation.
>
> _____
>
> _____
>
> _____

The *Conversation Worksheet* will give you the raw ingredients you need to talk to anyone, when used in combination with some specific, teachable conversation skills. Let's look at these skills in detail:

Skill #1: Use a Good Opening

How do you start a conversation? Simple:

1) Use the other person's name once
2) Ask this person how they are.

Now suppose that you do this, and they respond and say, "I'm fine, thanks." Now what? This is where you use one of the 3-5 prepared conversation starters from your worksheet, about things that normally interest most people. Here are some examples:

- "What are you up to these days?"
- "How is work/school/their band/their favorite project/etc. going?"
- "How is your partner/family doing?"
- "What have you been up to this summer?"

Once they answer, sit back, relax, and listen to what they have to say. And then proceed to skill #2, to learn how to always know how to respond effectively.

Skill #2: Acknowledge What They Say

This is your secret weapon. Most people do not know how to really acknowledge other people. And this is probably the main reason you fear sitting in stunned silence when someone speaks to you.

Here is how you fix this problem: choose one of four "octane levels" of acknowledgement, each of which will make people heard and felt:

1. Paraphrasing: Interpret their words, and hand their thought right back to them.
- "So, school is going really well for you these days."
- "Sounds like you've met the girl/guy of your dreams."

2. Observation: Play back what they are feeling. P.S. It's perfectly OK to guess — they'll correct you if needed, and it's fine!
- "You must be incredibly frustrated about that"
- "I can tell by your tone of voice how much that mattered to you"
- "You must be really proud of finishing that."

3. Validation: Not only are you observing their feelings here, but telling them these feelings are valid — by comparing them to other people. So simply invite a big crowd into your answer first:

- "That really stinks! Hard drive crashes are devastating for just about everyone"
- "No one likes having to wait for the plumber to show up"
- "There is nothing like a cold beer and a hot slice of pizza on a summer night."

4. Identification: The best one of all. Respond by sharing how *you* would feel:
- "That would bother me too."
- "I'm thrilled when something like that happens to me"

Note that you can use any of these four forms of acknowledgement even when you disagree with what the other person is saying. *Acknowledgement is not the same as agreement.*

Use the worksheet to prepare specific acknowledgements based on what the other person might say to you. When you do a good job of acknowledging people, you will seem like the most engaged, interesting person in the world. People whom you think of as having "good people skills," more often than not, simply know how to acknowledge people better than others.

> ***TIP***: *Practice these skills on a videotaped conversation, such as dialogue on YouTube or television. They get much, much better with practice, and will substantially build your confidence.*

Skill #3: Ask Good Questions

Asking good questions shows interest in the other person. Where do you find material for good questions? Simple — the other person will usually hand it to you! For example:

He: "So I'm going to Florida this summer with my parents."
You: "Cool! What sights do you plan on visiting?"

She: "This was a really tough breakup for me."
You: "Sorry to hear. How are you taking care of yourself these days?"

Good questions show interest — and more important, they lob the ball back to the other person to continue the conversation. You can use the worksheet to prepare questions in advance, or simply follow the other person's lead.

Skill #4: Your Turn

Listening to and acknowledging other people are very powerful behaviors — but unless you put a little of yourself in the conversation, it can turn into an interrogation rather than a dialogue. So prepare 3-5 common things to say about yourself in the course of the conversation — either about you personally, or a topic of mutual interest. For example:

- "I'm planning to change my major in school this year."
- "I've met a nice person and we're trying to start a relationship."
- "How about those Mets! I hope they finally win the pennant this year."

- "I really enjoyed the latest episode of Mad Men this week."

You only need to start the conversation — then the ball goes back to them. And then you can keep acknowledging them, or add your own observations. Try to read their body language if you can — normally you will find that the other person is comfortably in dialogue with you.

How often should you talk about yourself? If you are comfortable speaking with someone, most satisfying conversations have a natural give-and-take that follows the rhythm of the dialogue. If you aren't comfortable yet, however, use the *three-to-one rule* — try to say something about yourself after every three things the other person says about him or herself.

This isn't a rigid rule, but rather a guideline to help you focus on creating meaningful conversation. Often you will find that people really like to talk about themselves, and you may have to wait for a good opening! Just remember that the goal is to engage the other person by both listening and sharing at least a little about yourself.

Skill #5: Welcome Silence

People with social anxiety fear silence. They presume it makes them look bad. In reality, comfortable periods of silence are part of the rhythm of any normal conversation. Relax, smile, and learn to be comfortable with increasingly longer periods of silence. And remember, it's up to the other person to speak as much as it is up to you!

Skill #6: Wrap It Up

Silence also serves a valuable function in dialogue — it lets both people know that the conversation has reached a logical stopping point. Whenever you are ready to break away — whether it is after just basic pleasantries or a longer dialogue — have 3-5 prepared phrases ready to end the conversation gracefully. For example:

- "It was great to see you again, Sally!"
- "Hopefully we'll catch up on campus again."
- "I have to run to a meeting now. Talk with you again soon!"

> *TIP: Psychologists know that we often judge experiences on the last things we hear. So leaving a conversation on a very positive note will usually cancel any negative or awkward impressions during the course of the conversation.*

Skill #7: Understand the Exceptions

Most conversations really do follow this simple formula: opening/acknowledgment, questions/ acknowledgement, and self-disclosure — followed by a good closing. But what if someone doesn't respond to your questions, or your acknowledgement, or respond to what you say?

    The answer is deceptively simple: relax, smile, and close the conversation early. Particularly when your conversational partner is an introvert, a strong positive closing will make them feel better too. Either way, this approach honors the other person's readiness and willingness to talk, which in turn leaves a good impression.

Each of these seven steps are *skills*. You can learn them and put them to use, like any job or social skill. The more you use them, the more confident you will feel — with no change in personality required. With time and practice, you can learn to become more comfortable in your interactions with other people, no matter who you are.

Today's Action Plan

- Understand that good conversation is an easily teachable skill
- Fill out the *Conversation Worksheet* to prepare how you might have a good, 5-7 minute conversation with someone
- Practice having a short conversation with someone who feels relatively "safe" to you, and then reflect on how this makes you feel

CHAPTER 12

Dealing with Family and Friends

No man (or woman) is an island: most of us live in a social context that involves friends, family members, and our interactions with others. When someone suffers from anxiety, it often involves their entire social system: your anxiety disorders affect them, and the things they say and do affect you as well.

- People's attitudes towards anxiety can have a great impact on you as a sufferer. Some people are supportive, others feel anxiety sufferers should "pull their socks up" and get over it (which no one can do, by the way).
- People often fail to realize that anxiety is a real, physical illness, treated by behavioral and/or medical means.
- Conversely, the constraints and limitations of an anxiety sufferer often severely impact relationships with friends and family.
- The people in your life can be important allies in healing anxiety.
- Teamwork, authentic dialogue, and gradually negotiated boundaries can make life much easier for everyone.

This chapter looks at specific communications skills that can help take the anxiety out of your interactions with people in your own social circle. Knowing what to say in difficult situations like these is not a matter of being "smarter," or being able to think quickly on your feet - it is a set of skills that anyone can learn and practice.

Disclosing an Anxiety Disorder

When you describe an anxiety disorder to someone you know - such as a relative, a friend, or a supervisor - it can be awkward and uncomfortable. But the right words can help make it easier on both sides.

Before you decide what to say, decide whether to disclose. Sadly, some people still have dated stereotypes about mental illness, and discrimination still exists. Consider also whether your struggles with anxiety are as visible to others as they are to you - many people are often surprised to learn that someone they know struggles with anxiety.

If you decide to disclose an anxiety disorder, here are some things you can share:

- That you are not "crazy" or emotionally unstable
- That you suffer from a neurological problem that affects millions of people in the United States
- That you are seeking effective treatment for this issue
- That you appreciate their support

From there, the other person's reaction will guide your responses. Do your best to understand whatever they say, with respect and dignity for both them and yourself.

Finally, remember that disclosing an anxiety disorder is a very personal decision. Disorders such as these are part of your personal health information, and as such, are protected by law. It is your decision whether to disclose anything – or nothing at all – about any aspect of your physical or mental health.

> ***Exercise: Setting the Record Straight***
>
> *You are at a family gathering, with a number of relatives you haven't seen in a long time. As you walk through the kitchen on your way to the bathroom, you overhear your Uncle Louie mentioning your name to some of the other relatives and saying, "You know, it's really too bad about her these days. She's gone kind of ... you know ... coo-coo lately," as he circles his finger around his forehead.*
>
> *As he finishes talking, many of the other relatives laugh and nod their heads - and then everyone turns around to see you, and falls silent. Uncle Louie is visibly red-faced. Answer the following questions:*
>
> *1) Would you say something?*
>
> *2) These are distant relatives who live in a faraway city, and you may not get the chance to see them again for a long time. What kinds of things might you say to set the record straight?*
>
> *3) What might you say to Uncle Louie?*

Sometimes anxiety itself can revolve around not knowing what to say to people we know. We worry that we will be "caught" without the right words, and be embarrassed or humiliated. But these are often procedural skills that can be learned and practiced, to help strengthen ourselves. Common situations include:

- How to respond when people challenge us
- What to say when someone notices something embarrassing
- What to say in response to an unexpected compliment

Let's look at each of these in detail.

When People Challenge Us

In situations like this, we often dread getting into a verbal tug-of-war, as they say things that upset us and we fight back defending ourselves. But as the character Obi-Wan Kenobi once said in the movie Star Wars, "there are alternatives to fighting."

The key to managing situations like these is to take the other person's power away by finding ways to agree with them. This does not mean groveling or losing our dignity - rather, it means making it clear to the other person that we alone decide how we react to criticism. Here are a couple of examples:

Them: You are always acting out!
You: I can be a handful sometimes.

Them: You are pretty strange these days.
You: I do act differently sometimes, because of a treatable anxiety disorder that I am still working on.

The key here is to acknowledge what the other person says, while keeping your dignity. This goes against our human nature, where our first instinct is to defend ourselves. By "leaning in" to challenges like these, we gain credibility, and make it much more likely that people will listen to how we honestly feel about whatever they bring up.

When Someone Notices Something Embarrassing

Mark Twain once said, " You stop worrying about what other people think about you when you realize how little they do." Yet many of us live in fear of being "noticed" by others.

You can strengthen yourself against these situations by knowing how to respond when they happen:

- Acknowledge the other person
- Do not defend yourself
- Do not put yourself or the other person down
- Keep a sense of humor if at all possible

For example:

Peter Picky: I see you're always taking forever to wash your hands in the rest room!
You: You're right, I am a bit of a clean freak. Germs don't stand a chance with me!

Responding to an Unexpected Compliment

Sometimes unexpected compliments can be embarrassing, and we worry what to say - will we clam up, or babble on, or tell people we are somehow unworthy?

This is perhaps the simplest situation to handle, because when it happens, all you need to do is smile and thank them. That's it!

> **Exercise: Your Friend the Nitpicker**
>
> Your friend Tillie Tally is a nitpicker who needs to have everything done exactly her way - but when it comes to your own anxieties around people or situations, she has no empathy at all, telling you to "buck up and get over it."
>
> You like Tillie's company, because she is smart and funny, and you both share common interests - but this lack of empathy, even as you accommodate her peccadilloes, is really starting to bother you.
>
> What might you say to Tillie? And in particular, what can you say that might keep her from getting on the defensive and dropping you as a friend?

Making It Safe to Talk About Your Anxiety

Now, what about situations where you want to speak up to people you know? You may want to address how you are viewed or treated, clear up misunderstandings about your needs, or set better expectations. But unless you are careful, these conversations can easily put people on the defensive and go off the rails – especially with the people you are closest to. Here are four steps that can help you make it safe to talk about your anxiety issues to people you care about:

Step 1: Start the discussion in a safe place. Start the conversation with neutral observations or questions that are (a) on-topic, but (b) do not put the other person on the defensive - even when you feel frustrated toward the other person. Here are some examples:

Not safe	Safe
You won't ever talk to me.	Is it uncomfortable for you to talk about this?
You make me feel really stupid about behaviors I can't always help.	I realize that my behavior doesn't always follow the same rules yours does.
You don't have any empathy for what I am going through.	I realize that it is hard to understand my behavior sometimes.
You are always stabbing me in the back.	Sometimes you share your frustrations about me with other people. Can we talk about it?

Step 2: Acknowledge the other person. Next, and most important, remember four "octane levels" of acknowledgement we discussed in the previous chapter: paraphrasing what the other person says, observing how they are feeling, validating their feelings as legitimate (even when you don't agree with them), or identifying with their views. Where possible, try to acknowledge them every time they open their mouth.

Step 3: Discuss your concerns factually instead of emotionally. When you start in a safe place and acknowledge the other person, you can be extremely frank - as long as you are factual and not critical. For example:

- It is sometimes hard for me to do everything you expect.
- I feel hurt when you say things like X.
- I would like to work together better in the future with you on this.
- When you criticize my behavior about things that are difficult for me, I feel alone and hurt.

- It would mean a lot to me if you noticed when I make small changes. Sometimes those changes were very brave for me to make.

Step 4: Engage the other person with good questions. Most of us think about what to tell the other person, when in reality we should be thinking about what to ask them. Here are some examples of good questions that take a learning stance:

- Where can we go from here?
- How could I best support you in the future?
- Given how we both feel, what would be fair for everyone?
- What could we change so that we both feel respected from here?

The greater principle here is to make it safe for the other person to hear you, while being assertive about what you need. It is a win-win for both parties when no one feels shamed, and everyone learns. When you learn to engage people close to you and have frank, productive conversations with them, you not only increase your chances of getting what you want – you are much more likely to build partnerships based on mutual respect.

Today's Action Plan

- It is your decision whether to disclose an anxiety disorder. If you do choose to disclose, present it factually as a real, physical illness that you would like the other person's support for.
- Understand that anxiety disorders are real illnesses that affect the entire family - that should be treated with the

respect of a real illness by all parties, as partners in recovery.
- When you are challenged or ridiculed, learn not to fight back, defend yourself, or criticize the other person. Instead, acknowledge the other person and speak respectfully about yourself and your boundaries.

CHAPTER 13

Beyond Your Mind: Other Approaches

When I worked for a major aerospace company in the 1980s, there was a humorous poster showing how different groups at this company would design an airplane. For example, the propulsion group's plane had a tiny body and two huge engines, while the loft group (which designed the shape of the airplane) had a plane consisting of two boards nailed together. It was a joke, of course, but it was funny because there was some truth in jest: we all tend to see things through the lens of our own interests.

A similar situation holds true for anxiety disorders. As a psychotherapist, I tend to believe that psychotherapy is a dandy way to treat anxiety. A physician may be more likely to look at the impact of medication on these issues. An exercise physiologist may first point you towards the gym. Still others might have you wearing a white robe and meditating in front of a candle.

The purpose of this chapter is to briefly discuss some of the additional strategies people use for managing anxiety disorders. These include medication, nutrition, exercise, and other approaches. Any or all of these strategies may serve as an important complement to the approaches we discuss in this book, and help form part of a more holistic approach to dealing with your fears.

Medication

Medications for anxiety have a long history: there is even evidence of prehistoric societies using psychoactive substances over 10,000 years ago! Today, prescription psychiatric medications are often among the best selling drugs on the market. Some of the more common types include:

Benzodiazepines: Popularly known as "tranquilizers," these drugs often have anti-anxiety and anti-panic properties, and generally function as muscle relaxants with sedative and/or hypnotic properties.

SSRIs/SNRIs: These latest generations of antidepressant medication affect the balance in the brain of neurotransmitter chemicals such as serotonin and/or norepinephrine (Their acronyms stand for "selective serotonin reuptake inhibitor" and "serotonin-norepinephrine reuptake inhibitor" respectively.) These are also often used to treat anxiety.

Other anti-anxiety medications: Antihistamine drugs (some of which are specifically formulated for anxiety relief), beta-blockers (blood pressure medications that also prevent shaking and tremors, and are often used for performance anxiety) and other drugs are sometimes prescribed for anxiety relief. In addition, medicines designed to manage symptoms of more serious mental illnesses also may have an impact on anxiety.

I personally have a cautious view of using medication for anxiety. In my own experience, treating several hundred patients for anxiety, I see a wide range of outcomes. Many people feel that appropriate use of medication has given them their life back, and are thankful that these medicines are available. Others struggle with the side effects of psychiatric medications, sometimes with the result that they end up trying different meds or even giving up entirely.

Still others – thankfully a minority – have found themselves developing a tolerance or dependence for medications with regular use, particularly among the benzodiazepine family. For example, I personally developed a dependence on a benzodiazepine sleeping medication during my early struggles with agoraphobia decades ago: it worked extremely well at first, but terminating it gave me worse anxiety than ever, and I eventually ended up tapering off of it over a six-month period.

The subject of medication often stirs up strong opinions among people, and even among practitioners. Some people are opposed to their use, others favor using them with caution, and still others are strong proponents of their use. In addition, your particular diagnosis is often a factor: for example, some people may use medication on an as-needed basis for stressful situations, while others with serious and persistent mental illnesses such as bipolar disorder or schizophrenia often use medication as an important part of their strategy for day-to-day functioning.

Another important factor in the decision to use medication is your own personal beliefs and attitudes about it. Personally, I feel it would be cruel to press medications on people who are not comfortable taking them, and equally cruel to deny them to people who feel they want and need them. Perhaps the most important advice I can give regarding medication and anxiety is to learn all you can about possible medications – including benefits, side effects, and recommended usage – and then discuss your needs with a competent prescriber who listens and builds trust with you.

Nutrition

You are what you eat – particularly when you are anxious or suffer from fears. Nutritional stressors can be a significant and often hidden source of discomfort for anxiety sufferers, and the mind-body connection between your physical well-being and your mental health is often a key factor in anxiety disorders.

Sugar. When someone suffers from chronic anxiety, one of the first things I will assess is their daily diet – and it is not unusual for us to discover an excess of refined sugar may be part of the equation. This often extends to much more than obvious sweet foods such as desserts: soft drinks, cereals such as granola, and snacks such as protein bars may also contain large amounts of sugar. The problem with foods like these is that they can cause a sharp rise in blood sugar, followed by a mood-destroying crash leaving you shaky and anxious.

Caffeine. It is one of the world's most popular stimulant drugs, and many people make a running joke about being miserable without their daily dose of coffee – but for some people, particularly with anxiety, caffeine is no joke and they are very sensitive to its effects. Coffee, tea and caffeinated sodas all can cause or exacerbate anxiety in susceptible people, and many people find that their mood improves when they eliminate caffeine from their diet.

Processed foods. In addition to often being high in refined sugars and flours, processed foods often contain preservatives or other ingredients that exacerbate anxiety. For example, one recent study linked high levels of sodium benzoate, a common preservative, to anxiety in laboratory animals.

A good strategy for eating for better mental health is to first listen to your body, and pay attention to how you feel after the things you normally eat. Then try making gradual changes toward a healthier diet, perhaps with the assistance of a dietician or nutritionist, and see how these changes affect your mood. In general, eating right can become a strong positive factor in your resilience to anxiety.

Physical Activity

There is now a well-established link between physical exercise and lower levels of anxiety and depression. Exercise releases endorphins that contribute to an improved mood, and appropriate levels of physical activity will improve your general physical and cognitive functioning. Current US government guidelines for physical activity recommend that adults do at least 150 minutes of moderate-intensity activity per week, 75 minutes of vigorous-intensity activity, or a combination of both.

The Anxiety and Depression Association of America (ADAA) recommends taking an approach to exercise that dovetails well with cognitive-behavioral therapy for your fears: set small goals, consider working with an "exercise buddy" to provide motivation to stick with it, and be patient and give the process time. I would also add to be sure and consult with your physician before beginning any exercise program, particularly if you have been sedentary or out of shape for a long time.

Other Strategies

Mankind has come up with numerous strategies for dealing with fears and anxiety throughout the course of history, and many of them have surprisingly stood the test of time. For example, the ancient Greeks addressed anxiety using concepts of Stoic philosophy and logic that could be seen as precursors to today's cognitive-behavioral therapy, while many Chinese traditional medicine approaches dating back over 2000 years are still in use today as well.

The fields of alternative and complementary medicine often devote their efforts to the relief of emotional stress, and some of my own patients have used techniques ranging from herbal supplements and acupuncture to aromatherapy to help themselves feel better. In their minds, good medicine does not always take place in the confines of a medical or psychiatric journal, and natural approaches make more sense to them.

My own view? I am originally an engineer by training, so my preferences lie towards evidence-based strategies that are published in the literature. Some alternative treatments may have only tenuous or anecdotal evidence to support them, and the success of some may spring from the placebo effect, where the effects of a treatment spring largely from your belief in it. I would also caution people that many "natural" treatments still have the potential for harm and/or side effects, so I feel it is important to be an educated consumer and get professional advice for anything you might try.

That said, I am also in favor of whatever works for people, and even the United States government now has a division of the National Institutes of Health exploring alternative medicine: The National Center for Complementary and Integrative Health. By keeping an open mind, and doing homework from legitimate sources, you may find additional tools that help in your journey towards losing your fears.

Today's Action Plan

- Explore your feelings about medication, and whether it might be helpful in trying to overcome your anxieties.
- Examine your diet, and see if reducing nutritional stressors like refined sugar, caffeine and processed foods might improve your anxiety level.
- Consider developing an exercise regimen that you would be comfortable following regularly, and check with your physician first.

CHAPTER 14

Life Beyond Anxiety

You made it. You have successfully recovered from your fears and phobias. Now you are doing things you never thought you could before, and it feels wonderful. So how will things go from here?

When I first recovered from my own agoraphobia, it was truly amazing. If I read about an event or a nice restaurant out of town, I could actually go there. Crossing a state line, which at one point would have seemed as unreachable as going to the moon, was now an exciting new discovery. I'll never forget pushing back tears of joy at my first ride on a jumbo jet, or setting foot in Mexico soon after my recovery. Within the next few years, my wife and I even traveled overseas to Europe and Asia, visiting sights and having life experiences we would have never dreamed of.

But I would be lying to say that it was a pure, unadulterated life of happily-ever-after. Leaving home soon brought on all the pressures of a professional career. I quickly discovered that my mood still had good days and bad days, like everyone. To my horror, I even had a setback where I went running home from a week-long business trip, after letting myself get too exhausted and not taking care of myself. But eventually life and its lessons went on, and today I generally look in the mirror and see a pretty normal and happy person looking back.

So what is life really like as you recover from an anxiety disorder? Here are some practical guidelines for what to expect:

1. The absence of anxiety is not bliss: it is life

Frank Sinatra once said, "I've been rich and I've been poor, and baby, rich is better." So it is with anxiety: life without it is much better than life with it. At the same time, it would be a mistake to presume that losing an anxiety disorder guarantees a state of never-ending bliss.

When you recover from an anxiety disorder, you will discover that you still have the right to be bored, lonely, happy, or any of the other real emotions that come with life experiences – including some anxiety once in a while! All our emotions have real purposes that are triggered by all the real things that happen in our lives. Yet these emotions may feel strange after years or even decades of constantly being on alert from an anxiety disorder. So be prepared to learn a new "reality" as you expand your boundaries, and be present within this new reality.

2. Setbacks are normal

You go for months feeling "cured," and then WHAM! - one day you feel like you are anxious again and back to square one.

Relax. Literally, and figuratively. You had bad days before you developed an anxiety disorder, and you will have them after you recover from one. An anxiety episode after recovery can have many causes: high levels of stress in your life, mind-body issues, hyperventilation, or lingering subconscious fears, to name just a few. And they happen to just about everyone.

Use anxiety setbacks to assess what is going on in your life, physically or emotionally, and don't be afraid to see your therapist or physician to discuss these issues further - preferably sooner rather than later. And remember that the same tools that helped you get well the first time will help you get well again.

3. Keep measuring your progress

Ironically, how you feel is often a poor barometer of how much progress you are making, particularly at first. Why? Because feelings often lag functionality. As you face your fears and are able to accomplish more, it is not unusual to still subjectively feel anxious until these new skills become routine for you.

Keep using instruments such as the Generalized Anxiety Disorder Scale (GAD-7) or the Yale-Brown Obsessive Compulsive Scale (Y-BOCS) to measure your progress. Ideally, you should aim for reducing your score on both tests into the single digits - and when you reach this point, you will in all likelihood be feeling really good most of the time.

Here is another even simpler measure: how many of your days are good ones? As a short-term goal, you should aim for having more "good days" than "bad days." In the long term, in the absence of external stresses in your life, you should aim for having the majority of your days be good ones.

4. Set your standards high

Don't view yourself as a flawed individual who must always take better care of yourself. Your goal should be to wake up every morning feeling as normal as the next person - and with proper treatment and social support, this should be a reachable goal for most of us. The same tools that help you get from "suffering" to "functional" will also help you go much further, from "functional" to "normal" - and this should ultimately be your goal.

Have you been able to make progress on what is comfortable? Are there issues that are less of a problem for you now? Do you have moments of peace and clarity? Then you probably have all the ingredients you need within you for a happy and fulfilling life. Keep working on your goals, and don't ever settle for the label of being a quote-unquote "anxious person."

It is on this last point that we will close: namely, that you are not a label or a disorder. You are a talented, intelligent person with a finely-tuned survival instinct that is working A-OK. You are worthy of love and respect. And anxiety disorders are highly treatable issues that you can understand and manage with the aid of some new skills. Once you learn these skills, they are yours for a lifetime, and no one can ever take them away from you. Thank you for sharing part of your journey with me, and here's to the good life you should expect and deserve!

Bibliography

Introduction:
Smith, Manual J., *Kicking the Fear Habit*, Dial Press, 1977.

Chapter 1:
Psychiatric Times, An Ultra-Brief Screening Scale for Anxiety and Depression: the PHQ-4, http://www.psychiatrictimes.com/all/editorial/psychiatrictimes/pdfs/scale-PHQ4.pdf

Pfizer, Inc., Patient Health Questionnaire (PHQ) Screeners, http://www.phqscreeners.com/

Spitzer RL, Kroenke K, Williams JBW, Lowe B. A brief measure for assessing generalized anxiety disorder. Arch Inern Med. 2006;166:1092-1097

Patient, Generalised Anxiety Disorder Assessment (GAD-7), http://patient.info/doctor/generalised-anxiety-disorder-assessment-gad-7

Psychology Tools, Yale-Brown Obsessive Compulsive Scale, https://psychology-tools.com/yale-brown-obsessive-compulsive-scale/

Anxiety Disorders Association of America, http://www.adaa.org

Social Anxiety Institute, http://www.socialanxietyinstitute.org

Kessler RC, McGonagle KA, Zhao S, et al. Lifetime and 12-month prevalence of DSM-III-R psychiatric disorders in the United States: results from the National Comorbidity Survey. *Archives of General Psychiatry*. 1994;51:8–19.

Clark et al., "Temperament, Personality, and the Mood and Anxiety Disorders," *Journal of Abnormal Psychology*, 1994;103(1):103-116.

Janowsky DS, Morter S, Tancer M, "Over-representation of Myers Briggs Type Indicator introversion in social phobia patients," *Depression and Anxiety*. 2000;11(3):121-5.

United States Public Health Service, Office of the Surgeon General, *Mental Health: A Report of the Surgeon General*, National Institute of Mental Health, Washington DC, 1999.

Williams et al., *Evidence-Based Dermatology*, Wiley, New York, 2009.

"Spotlight On ... Roger Moore," *RedOrbit.com*, October 4, 2008, http://bit.ly/1s3Q4ks

Woodstock, Nicola, "Sir Roger admits to worst bout of stage fright," *The Telegraph (UK)*,

"Tony Shalhoub talks Monk (interview)," *The TV Addict*, May 15, 2008, http://bit.ly/1tNRTXa

"Fears and Phobias of 25 Big Celebrities," *AOL-HuffPost Entertainment*, http://bzfd.it/10cJIHY

Finkelstein, Jesse, "21 Celebrity Phobias That Will Make You Feel Better About Your Own Anxieties," *Buzzfeed.com*, June 27, 2013, http://bzfd.it/10cJIHY

Canadian Psychological Association, *The Efficacy and Effectiveness of Psychological Treatments*, 2013, http://www.cpa.ca/docs/File/Practice/TheEfficacyAndEffectivenessOfPsychologicalTreatments_web.pdf

Leung, Martin, "Knee Surgery: No Benefits in Mild Osteoarthritis," *General Surgery News*, September 2014, http://bit.ly/1qP5cQU

Chapter 3:

"Blood: A Touching, Unnecessary Sacrifice," The Encyclopedia of 9/11, *New York Magazine*, Aug. 27, 2011, http://nymag.com/news/9-11/10th-anniversary/blood-donations/

Chapter 4:

Wikipedia contributors, "Diaphragmatic Breathing," accessed April 4, 2017, http://en.wikipedia.org/wiki/Diaphragmatic_breathing.

Cuncic, Arlin, How to Practice Progressive Muscle Relaxation, http://socialanxietydisorder.about.com/od/copingwithsad/qt/pmr.htm

Alstetter, William, Panic Attacks and "Suffocation Alarm Systems," http://www.cumc.columbia.edu/news/journal/journal-o/archives/jour_v19no1/theories.html

Soultherapynow, "Breathing Exercises," http://soultherapynow.com/articles/breathing-exercises.html

Salcedo, Dr. Beth, *Progressive Muscle Relaxation* (MP3 download), http://www.amazon.com/Progressive-Muscle-Relaxation/dp/B001AJRNJG

Progressive Muscle Relaxation, http://www.wikieducator.org/Stress_management_modalities/Progressive_muscle_relaxation

University of Texas' Mind-Body Lab, http://www.cmhc.utexas.edu/mindbodylab.html

U.S. Department of Veterans' Affairs, "Relaxation Exercise: Deep Breathing," http://www.va.gov/vetsinworkplace/docs/em_eap_exercise_breathing.asp

Chapter 5:

Mayo Clinic, "Panic Attacks and Panic Disorder," http://www.mayoclinic.org/diseases-conditions/panic-attacks/basics/risk-factors/con-20020825

Strayhorn, Joseph Mallory, *A Programmed Course in Anxiety Reduction and Courage Skills: Reducing Obsessions, Compulsions, Aversions, and Fears*, Psychological Skills Press, Wexford, PA, Jan. 2012.

Weekes, Claire. *Hope and Help for Your Nerves*. Signet, New York, 1969.

Chapter 7:

Wikipedia contributors, "Guided Imagery," accessed April 4, 2017, https://en.wikipedia.org/wiki/Guided_imagery

Tull, Matthew PhD, "Imagery Rehearsal Treatment for Nightmares Related to PTSD," *Verywell.com*, April 22, 2016, https://www.verywell.com/imagery-rehearsal-treatment-for-nightmares-2797657

Strayhorn, Joseph Mallory, *A Programmed Course in Anxiety Reduction and Courage Skills: Reducing Obsessions, Compulsions, Aversions, and Fears*, Psychological Skills Press, Wexford, PA, Jan. 2012.

Chapter 12:

Bullies2Buddies (website), http://www.bullies2buddies.com/

Gallagher, Richard S., *How to Tell Anyone Anything: Breakthrough Techniques for Handling Difficult Conversations at Work*, New York: Amacom, 2009.

Ross, Jerilyn, *Triumph Over Fear: A Book of Help and Hope for People with Anxiety*, Panic Attacks and Phobias, New York: Bantam, 1995.

Anxiety Disorders Association of America, "Helping a Family Member," http://www.adaa.org/GettingHelp/HelpAFamilyMember.asp

Ginott, Haim G., *Between Parent and Child*, New York: Three Rivers Press, 1965 (Revised edition 2003).

Obsessive Compulsive Foundation, " Living with Someone Who Has OCD: Guidelines for Family Members" by Barbara Livingston Van Noppen, Ph.D. and Michele Tortora Pato, MD, Spring 2009 newsletter, http://www.ocfoundation.org/UserFiles/File/OCF_Newsletter/OCF_Newsletter_v23_n2_Spring_2009.pdf

Chapter 13:

Gray, Richard, "No wonder they called it the stone age! Ancient humans were taking drugs - including magic mushrooms and opium - up to 10,600 years ago," *Daily Mail*, February 4, 2015, http://www.dailymail.co.uk/sciencetech/article-2939830/No-wonder-called-stone-age-Ancient-humans-taking-drugs-including-magic-mushrooms-opium-10-600-years-ago.html

Anxiety.org, "Processed foods high in sodium benzoate aggravate anxiety," November 22, 2017, https://www.anxiety.org/the-top-five-foods-that-are-making-you-anxious-preservatives

Crocq, Marc-Antoine MD, "A history of anxiety: from Hippocrates to DSM," *Dialogues in Clinical Neuroscience*. September 2015; 17(3): 319–325. https://www.ncbi.nlm.nih.gov/pmc/articles/PMC4610616/

Kecskes, Alex A., "Anxiety Disorders and Traditional Chinese Medicine," Pacific College of Oriental Medicine blog, October 4, 2014. http://www.pacificcollege.edu/news/blog/2014/10/04/anxiety-disorders-and-traditional-chinese-medicine

Office of Disease Prevention and Health Promotion (health.gov), *2008 Physical Activity Guidelines for Americans Summary*, https://health.gov/paguidelines/guidelines/summary.aspx

Anxiety and Depression Association of America, "Exercise for Stress and Anxiety," updated July 2014. https://www.adaa.org/living-with-anxiety/managing-anxiety/exercise-stress-and-anxiety

National Institutes of Health, National Center for Complementary and Integrative Health, https://nccih.nih.gov/

ABOUT THE AUTHOR

Rich Gallagher, LMFT, is a practicing psychotherapist and a bestselling communication skills author. He specializes in the treatment of anxiety disorders and developed the Anxiety Camp program in 2009, an intensive group program for anxiety sufferers and their families that is now also a certified continuing education program for licensed psychotherapists in New York State. He is a clinical fellow of the American Association of Marriage and Family Therapists, and served on the board of Cayuga Addiction Recovery Services.

    A former customer service executive and communications skills expert as well as a therapist, Rich is the author of nine previous books including *The Customer Service Survival Kit* (AMACOM, 2013), which launched at #1 in customer service on Amazon.com, the Amazon top 10 career skills book *How to Tell Anyone Anything* (AMACOM, 2009) and *What to Say to a Porcupine* (AMACOM, 2008), a business fable collection that reached #1 in customer service and business humor and was a finalist for 800-CEO-READ's Business Book of the Year. His books have been published in seven languages.

    Rich has spoken to audiences nationwide, keynoted national conferences and conducted numerous training programs. He has been featured on CNN.com, Time Magazine, BusinessWeek, AOL, MSN, the New York Post, morning drive radio, and other media outlets. He has also served as the subject matter expert for the American Management Association's Communication Bootcamp program as well as his own extensive communications skills courseware. Visit Rich at www.anxietycamp.com.

Appendix – Worksheets

The Mindfulness Trifecta

Write down how you might apply these three steps towards a situation you fear:

Step 1. Observe your thoughts and feelings. (Describe them through the words of a compassionate and neutral observer.)

_____
_____
_____

Step 2. Ground yourself in the present. (Use breath awareness, body awareness, or getting in touch with your senses and surroundings.)

_____
_____
_____

Step 3. Make a wise decision. (Don't just react to your thoughts and feelings — instead, pause, reflect, and then thoughtfully choose a course of action)

_____
_____
_____

Diaphragmatic Breathing Exercise[4]

1. Sit comfortably or lie down.
2. Place one hand on your stomach and one hand on your chest.
3. Breathe in slowly through your nose.
4. Feel your stomach expand as you inhale. If you are breathing from the stomach, the hand on your chest shouldn't move.
5. Focus on filling up your lower lungs with air.
6. Slowly exhale, releasing all the air out through your mouth.
7. Use your hand to feel your stomach fall as you exhale.
8. Practice breathing four to six breaths per minute (about one full inhale and exhale per 10-15 seconds).

Repeat this procedure up to 10 times. Most people experience a sense of calm and peace as they focus on their in-breath and their out-breath. However, if at any time during this exercise you feel lightheaded or uncomfortable, simply stop and resume normal breathing.

---

[4] Source: U.S. Dept. of Veterans' Affairs, "Relaxation Exercise: Deep Breathing," http://www.va.gov/vetsinworkplace/docs/em_eap_exercise_breathing.asp

Progressive Muscle Relaxation Exercise

Note: Consult important medical precautions in Chapter 4 of this book before attempting this exercise, particularly if you suffer from health issues or injuries.

Silently say the word "RELAX" as you breathe in and tense each muscle group, and then say "LET GO" as you breathe out and let these muscle groups go limp. Step by step, go through each of the following muscle groups:

- Toes – curl them towards you as you tighten them
- Feet and ankles – tighten these gradually. Note: if you start to get a cramp in the arch of your feet, press them flat against the floor.
- Calves – point your toes away from or towards you as you tighten these
- Thighs – squeeze both thighs together
- Buttocks – clench your cheeks together
- Lower back – gently and gradually tense your lower back muscles, and be cautious if you suffer from lower back pain
- Middle and upper back – gently arch your back to get in touch with these muscles, which are a key to relaxing your entire body
- Lower abdomen – tense the smooth muscles in your belly
- Chest and upper abdomen – bring your shoulders to the front to help tense these muscles
- Shoulders – lift your shoulders toward your ears as you tense them
- Upper arms
- Forearms and hands – make a fist as you tense these muscles
- Neck – gently rotate your head as you tense your neck muscles

- Face – make a big smile, hard enough to feel the corners of your mouth tensing up
- Eyes – close your eyes tightly
- Forehead – raise your eyebrows and try to get in touch with those hard-to-reach muscles in your upper scalp

Worksheet for Changing Fearful Thoughts

Step 1. Write down your fearful thought.

_____
_____
_____

Step 2. Write down what common distortions (e.g. errors in thinking) might be in this thought, including *exaggeration*, *prediction*, and *expectation*.

_____
_____
_____

Step 3. Rewrite this thought so that these distortions are no longer true.

_____
_____
_____

Reframing Worksheet

1. List some of the self-talk phrases you tell yourself about your fears.

2. How can you *reframe* the language of these phrases to be less scary? (For example, change "This is going to be a disaster" to "This is not what I would prefer")

3. How might you add more *agency* to your self-talk? (For example, "Here is what I will do next" or "I can cope with this")

Gradual Exposure Hierarchy

Create a list of feared situations, ranked in order of their subjective units of discomfort (SUDS) from 0 (lowest) to 100 (highest).

Use this hierarchy to direct your exposure practice, starting at the lowest level, and expanding as you become more comfortable. Remember to **start in your comfort zone, stay in your comfort zone, and see where you take your comfort zone from week to week**.

SUDS (0-100)	Situation

Exposure Practice Log

Log your daily exposure practices here, to track your progress in facing fearful situations.

Date	Situation	Initial SUDS	Ending SUDS

The Conversation Worksheet

1. List 3-5 prepared conversation starters:

_____
_____
_____

2. List the three most likely things for the person you are conversing with to say in response, and how you will acknowledge these:

_____
_____
_____

3. List three questions you can ask the other person:

_____
_____
_____

4. List 3-5 things you can say about yourself:

_____
_____
_____

5. List 3-5 prepared "closing phrases" to gracefully exit a conversation.

_____
_____
_____

Printed in Great Britain
by Amazon